"Sean and Thora are simply the best at what they do. When I wanted the best in their field I sent my team out to get them and didn't stop until we made a deal with them. They are great people and great business leaders!"

—BOB PARSONS, FOUNDER OF GODADDY

"In the time that I have known Sean and Thora, I have been impressed with their business acumen, entrepreneurial spirit, and integrity. While it is no small feat to be successful and trustworthy like Sean and Thora, it is something special."

—TOM WHALLEY, CHIEF LABEL EXECUTIVE OF CONCORD RECORDS AND FORMER CEO OF WARNER BROS.

"Sean and Thora Dowdell are the true definition of business disruptors. Brand Renegades *is an eye-opening, page-turning book that will give you the inspiration and courage to step outside of the norm and make a big impact in your industry. I highly recommend this book to anyone that's ready to take their business to the next level of success!"*

—DEBBIE ALLEN, BUSINESS MENTOR AND BESTSELLING AUTHOR OF *SUCCESS IS EASY*

BRAND
RENEGADES

OUR FEARLESS PATH
FROM STARTUP TO
GLOBAL BRAND

SEAN AND THORA DOWDELL

Entrepreneur Press®

Entrepreneur Press, Publisher
Cover Design: Andrew Welyczko
Production and Composition: Eliot House Productions

This publication is designed to provide accurate and authoritative information
in regard to the subject matter covered. It is sold with the understanding that
the publisher is not engaged in rendering legal, accounting, or other professional
services. If legal advice or other expert assistance is required, the services of a
competent professional person should be sought.

Entrepreneur Press® is a registered trademark of Entrepreneur Media, Inc.

An application to register this book for cataloging has been submitted to the
Library of Congress.

ISBN 978-1-64201-122-7 (paperback) | ISBN 978-1-61308-443-4 (ebook)

Printed in the United States of America

25 24 23 22   10 9 8 7 6 5 4 3 2 1

CONTENTS

INTRODUCTION

We are entrepreneurs who currently own 13 successful businesses. We have been in business since 1995 and currently have more than 100 employees. Our largest company is Club Tattoo, a luxury tattoo and piercing studio chain that grosses more than $12 million annually and continues to expand. We have retail locations in some of the most successful and sought-after properties in the U.S., such as the Grand Canal Shoppes at The Venetian Resort, Miracle Mile Shops at the Planet Hollywood Resort & Casino, The LINQ Hotel + Experience, and the 5th Avenue shopping district in Scottsdale, Arizona, just to name a few. We have done global business collaborations with brands such as

Caesars Entertainment, Sole Technology/Etnies shoes, Jarden/Oster, Bicycle Playing Cards, and many more. This is just a sample of our business resume, but it gives you an idea of who we are and how we got here.

After 23 years of marriage (as of 2021), two children, several homes, 13 companies, and well over 100 employees, it is a wonderful feeling to share our story with other entrepreneurs. We have been quite successful and will share some of those successes with you throughout this book. However, we believe the more interesting parts of our story are told through our failures, our challenges, and how we dealt with them. Sometimes our reactions were intuitive; other times they were emotional and ended up not working out so well. In any case, we hope you find our story inspiring, uplifting, and at least interesting.

We both grew up in the 1970s under the Jimmy Carter administration, during one of the worst economic climates the United States has ever seen. Both of us had parents who worked full time and were what was then known as "latchkey children." We learned at a young age to be independent thinkers and understood that if we wanted something, we had to create the opportunity to get it. We chose the entrepreneur's path of going out and creating it for ourselves. Through hard work and perseverance, we would create businesses worth tens of millions of dollars, employ thousands of people over the years, and make a meaningful impact not only on our industry, but on our community as well.

> THORA: *I grew up in a small town called Price, Utah. It was a small coal mining community with a population of about 8,500, in which the "haves" and the "have nots" were completely segregated. Although my extended family was quite large, with many cousins, uncles, aunts, etc., my nuclear family was small. It was just me, my mother Willie Lue, my father Geno, and my brother Jason.*
>
> *My mother and father divorced when I was 7 years old, and my brother and I were given a choice of which parent*

we wanted to live with. It seemed like a cruel choice to give a child, but I understand that at the time they were doing what they thought was best. After all, back then there were not as many resources to help people cope with difficult situations. I chose my mother, and Jason chose our father.

Once our families were separated, my mother struggled to provide for us throughout my upbringing. While holding down a full-time job, she also worked as a waitress on the side to help support us. We lived in a low-income housing development just outside town that was nicknamed Divorce Alley, due to the many single women with children who lived there. She did her best, and I became the person I am today through many of the tough lessons I had to go through while growing up under those circumstances. I believe my drive to succeed was created through watching my mother's sheer determination to never give up and always get up and try again.

SEAN: *I also grew up in a blue-collar family with two hardworking parents, Kip and Kathy, along with my brother Kelly, and sister Shannan, in Phoenix, Arizona. I had a small extended family, limited to a few cousins, one aunt, and two uncles. My strongest family bonding memories are with my grandparents. My grandmothers, Lois and Editha, along with my grandfather, Russell, were hugely influential in my upbringing and helped create what would become my determination to build special things.*

Both my mother and father demonstrated the importance of a strong work ethic when I was growing up. I think I only saw them take four or five sick days (this is probably an exaggeration, but it's how I remember them) over my entire childhood. They worked hard every day and provided for us children the best they could.

We still struggled financially during my childhood, especially when my father left his job and went back to college to get his degree. I admire the courage it must have taken for my parents to tackle a challenge like that in the late 1970s and early 1980s. I always had a feeling of missing out on things as a child, whether it was the vacations my friends were going on, the clothes we couldn't afford, or the coolest new stereo to play our cassette tapes on. However, as I look back, we were always fed, clothed, and had a solid roof over our heads, along with parents who cared enough to push their children forward.

I got my work ethic from my parents, but I most certainly take after my grandfather in the way I approach business. I was around ten years old when he started teaching me about being an entrepreneur, talking about the printing business he had owned and operated back in Illinois. He had very fond memories of that time and always made running a business sound like an exciting adventure.

These simple conversations as a child would inspire me to become an entrepreneur myself and eventually go into business with my wife. We would create one of the most successful businesses in our industry and hopefully inspire other entrepreneurs to do the same.

When we went into business together, it wasn't really a conscious, strategic decision. At the time, it was simply a natural progression to our relationship. In the first few years, we fumbled through working together as best we knew how, often exploding into huge unnecessary fights that could have easily been avoided had we been willing to understand each other's perspectives.

To be completely honest, nearly all the early challenges and pain points were self-inflicted due to poor communication and lacking a basic understanding of what our roles should be in the operations of the company. Both of us were stubborn and young and thought we knew what was best in nearly any situation and did not understand the importance of acknowledging our weaknesses and holding ourselves accountable for our mistakes. It was unfathomable for us to admit when we were wrong and change direction or give in to each other's wishes—that felt like defeat rather than compromise and willingness to change based on better information or experience.

These were lessons we had to learn the hard way. Although we faced many such lessons in the early years of running our company together, we overcame each of our challenges because we never gave up and were always willing to work harder. Albeit at times, we were simply working harder and not smarter as we would learn later on.

WHAT TO EXPECT IN THIS BOOK

We wrote this book for entrepreneurs who need a little advice and encouragement, and who need to see that others have gone through and overcome similar challenges of building their businesses and brands. So many business books focus on huge corporations and deal with concepts that sometimes do not translate well into small business practices without a ton of stripping down. You don't have time to take apart Amazon's business practices or marketing strategies to see how you might apply a piece of that to your business. It's not practical for most people, and usually it doesn't scale down very well anyway.

Our purpose for writing this book is to offer real-world experience at a level that can be understood quickly and to offer lessons and solutions that can be applied to your own small business brand. We want to give you hope when things get tough. It is important for entrepreneurs to have someone they can relate to, who has faced the same issues and problems they are dealing with in their own business. We were lucky enough to have not only each other for support but also several other key mentors and friends who helped us push forward through the darkest times. Hopefully some of our experiences can help bring you clarity, and with that clarity you can overcome fear and become more focused and decisive. With decisiveness, you can take measured action, and with your actions there will come positive change.

Success as an entrepreneur has but one common element, and that is the will to work harder than almost anyone else. But we recognize that success also leaves clues (as Tony Robbins would say), and when we analyzed how our businesses became successful, we were able to measure many of the practices we implemented over the years. In this book, we will lay out many of the principles that we have taken from other businesses and some that we have developed for our business, and we will share our successes, failures, and pain points over the years so you too can become a true brand renegade.

Entrepreneurs are the only people crazy enough to quit a job working 40 hours a week for someone else, just so we can have the freedom to work 70 hours a week for ourselves. That is the strange logic by which we work every day. The freedom to choose our path is worth the sacrifice and extra work. It hasn't always been pretty, but for us, it has been a wonderful journey, and in the end, it was worth it. We hope you'll find it worthwhile, too.

1

OUR BRAND RENEGADE ORIGIN STORY

We were from completely different worlds until a third party's interference forced a meeting that would change our lives and an entire industry forever. What would lead a rock star and a corporate manager to think we could go into an industry perceived as dark, dirty, and disreputable and profit from flipping it on its ass? Some might even acknowledge we have played a major role in bringing this industry into a more mainstream existence.

And if that doesn't sound like enough of a challenge, try this on: We're not just business partners—we're also a married couple of 22 years who are raising two sons, Brennen and Carston. We both play full-out 24 hours a day, 7 days a week, 365 days a year in all aspects of life together. Don't be fooled, because we'll be the first ones to tell you it's not always pretty or easy. As a matter of fact, there are days that downright suck. We're two uniquely passionate, motivated, and opinionated people who bring different perspectives, temperaments, and skill sets to the business and the marriage.

But against the odds, as business partners, life partners, and parenting team, we are living the meaning of the words "Brand Renegades." We turned the tattoo and piercing industry inside out and built a thriving mainstream $30 million business empire. As of the end of 2019, we have six luxury locations of Club Tattoo in two states and manage more than 100 staff members.

We have survived the odds on multiple levels: 78 percent of small businesses fail in the first five years, and 50 percent of marriages fail in the first five years, too. Depending on which study you're reading, it's widely estimated that 25 to 70 percent of business partnerships also fail. But we simply don't care about the odds or how other people do things. As industry disruptors and brand renegades, we do business on our terms, on our timeline, and in our own way. We don't care that "it's never been done that way before." We don't care who gets angry or walks out, because we are ultimately secure in the fact that we're doing the right things by our standards in the way we conduct business, treat our employees, and care for our customers.

We were not reckless or irresponsible. Well, there were a few times we might have been a *little* bit reckless, but sometimes deciding to do something, even if the right answer isn't clear, is better than doing nothing at all. Sometimes it turned out well, and other times we lost millions of dollars. But we always learned something valuable about ourselves or the business from the experience. Meanwhile, other people were sitting around waiting for someone else to tell them what to do or how to do it. Or they were doing the same old thing for too little pay—or for no pay at all.

Here's a recent example of how we went against what others said was possible in a way that disrupted mainstream wisdom and standards in the industry. We wanted to open our first tattoo studio outside the Arizona market and decided to build one on the main Las Vegas Strip, inside Planet Hollywood's Miracle Mile Shops. Our feedback included comments like:

"You're going to lose millions."

"It won't work because it's never been done before."

"Tattoos can't compete with those other high-dollar, more respected businesses."

"You will never be able to pay those high-dollar rents and survive."

But think about it. The Strip is bright lights, excitement, 24-hour-a-day carefree fun. What comes to mind for businesses on the Strip, besides casino gambling? There are world-class stage shows, high-end restaurants, and designer brand stores. We felt there was a market void for experience-based shopping in the immediate market. Vegas had plenty of luxury shopping but very few immersive experiences that were attractive to the masses. We knew we could fill that void in a higher end/luxury atmosphere. In 2009, we added bright lights and a clean storefront that housed the newest flagship Club Tattoo location. It opened with three employees, six tattoo artists, and two body piercers; now it has 14 employees, 13 tattoo artists, and 3 professional body piercers.

This location was so successful that we nearly lost everything before we could get it established. When we opened the doors, there was a line as far as we could see of people wanting tattoos. We could not keep up with the demand. If this had been our first store, we would have crumbled under the sheer pressure. Given our experience, we thought we were prepared, but no way. We underestimated how successful this location was going to be, which is a good problem to have, but still a problem.

You want to kill a great business model? Provide a bad customer experience any day of the week, but especially on day one. Word-of-mouth will spread faster than you could imagine, especially in the current business world of Facebook, Google, and Yelp, where people can negatively impact your business with a few touches on their phone.

To overcome those initial challenges, we adjusted by working what felt like a million hours a week. Staffing was obviously a huge need. We had to quadruple our staff fast. We also had to figure out systems and processes for the new space and adjust for the different laws and code requirements in Nevada vs. Arizona. We had to rely on a lot of outside professional advice and make that fit into our business model in this new location.

Fortunately, we adjusted and responded quickly, which saved our business and reputations. But the nonstop demand prompted us to open a second studio in 2015 at another luxury Las Vegas location, The LINQ Hotel + Experience. These two locations are enormously successful, and the demand for tattoos, piercing, and the Club Tattoo lifestyle continues to grow.

Customer demand remained high enough, even after all these years, that in 2019, we opened a third Club Tattoo in The Venetian Resort. If we didn't do things on our terms, in our way, and on our timeline, we would have missed these opportunities. If we had listened to the people who said, "It's never been done," or "It can't be done," we would have watched someone else come along and do it.

Instead, we focused on our brand and how we could flip the script on what it means to grow a business. As brand renegades, we take bold action and are willing to take extreme risks to conduct business in a completely different way. We know when to ask the hard questions about our business and how to tell the difference between "Why?" and "Why not?"

With Las Vegas, it was a matter of "Why not do it?" What did we have to lose, rather than what did we have to gain? With our first store, we had to personally guarantee everything, so if it had failed, we may have lost our savings, our home, and other businesses. It was a huge risk. But on the other hand, if we succeeded, we would be creating something that hadn't existed in our industry up to that point. The obvious upside was the financial growth to us personally and professionally along with continued growth of the company. We took calculated risks to grow the Club Tattoo brand, and they paid off.

THORA: *[In other parts of the business], I just kept saying, "Why does it have to be like this?" I kept questioning. When Sean talked about our pricing, for example, I asked, "Why do we have to do it like that?" He knows I hate the answer, "Ah, well, that's the way it's always been done." That makes me want to find a way to do it, not just differently, but better!*

So, we look at everything and question: Why? Or why not? Is this the best way to do this or not? How can we make it better?

THE BRAND RENEGADE BLUEPRINT

As we built our business, it became clear that we had a unique opportunity to reset common perceptions of the tattoo and piercing industry and take our brand to a national level. To do that, we had to lean into a "brand renegade" mindset and apply it to our daily operations. To be a brand renegade, you have to take those standard views of your own business or industry and disrupt them to create a new brand identity. You have to both disrupt your industry and elevate your brand. So we decided not to seek approval from other people, question advice, and go with our ideas of how that input works or doesn't work for us. This means implementing different systems, processes, policies, and procedures than anyone else in the industry. We prioritized how to move the tattoo and piercing industries forward as a more mainstream, P&L-focused business by giving consideration to things like:

+ Updating health and safety policies, procedures, and standards
+ Using billing and appointment technology and automating as much as possible, even in calculating costs for the tattoo artwork
+ Assuring higher rates of payment and better treatment of the artists and other employees
+ Treating tattoo artists and body piercers like business assets who deserved to earn a respectable wage and be provided the supplies needed to do the job properly

+ Adding a quality retail outlet that enhanced the brand as a desirable "for sale" sideline, not as a marketing giveaway

+ Hiring people who might have little experience but a strong work ethic, providing solid training, and then getting out of the way to let them do their job

Some of these considerations are fairly commonplace in other industries, but they didn't exist within our industry and were massively disruptive.

We don't throw around that term—industry disruption—lightly. It tends to be used too frequently by people who are either full of hot air, don't know what the hell they're talking about, or both. Unless you're changing what everyone else in your industry is doing in some dramatic new way, you're simply not an industry disruptor—nor are you a brand renegade.

A brand renegade makes huge changes that everyone else turns their heads to notice, which makes a lot of other people in the industry uncomfortable and agitated. These emotions are nearly always rooted in fear. For example, the fear of falling behind their direct competitor's technology may lead a company's leaders to simply scoff at their competitors' innovations rather than truly examine what is being innovated and therefore analyzing the potential benefits to their own business model.

The other important quality of a brand renegade is success. A business owner can't be called a renegade if they shake up the marketplace, get media attention, have lines of customers for a week or two, but then close their doors forever because the risks they took led to bankruptcy. This is a flash-in-the-pan fad, not a true disruption fueled by a brand renegade. The successful brand renegade has staying power and causes others to ask, "What are they doing and how can we do it, too?"

Qualities of a Brand Renegade

Business owners who succeed in reframing their industries and elevating their brands doesn't just refer to new businesses coming into a marketplace and doing well. For example, it's not Kinko's coming in to compete with Copymax in the high-speed color copying business. It's not a new fast-food chain competing with three of the most successful disruptive chains: Subway, McDonald's, or KFC. The food served doesn't qualify any of these businesses as industry disruptors or brand renegades. It must have operations, structure, format, or other business functions that are dramatically different from any other fast-food chain on earth. A new business may take market share away from existing companies, but market share is not the same thing as turning an industry upside down in a distinctly successful, powerful way.

Examples of true industry disruptors that come to mind are:

- *Facebook*. Facebook was a latecomer to the online social media scene, but it took advantage of growing technology capabilities to reinvent how social connections were used. Then it disrupted the industry again with low-cost, closely targeted advertising. The disruption succeeded so well that it was the death knell for platforms like Friendster and Myspace. Facebook didn't just come in and take market share by connecting people online; it changed the way social media platforms functioned, attracted billions of users, and kept them engaged for longer periods of time.

- *Tesla*. Tesla is a company that came onto the business scene with a lot of promises that many of its competitors scoffed at or simply laughed off. The mission was to change the entire world with electric vehicle technology and slow the use of fossil fuels. Its CEO Elon Musk had a bold vision for his company right out of the gate and nearly went bankrupt in the process. Not only did his company end up riding out the financial storm and break the enormous barrier to invention and entry into the marketplace, but they have become the seventh-largest auto company in the world (and climbing fast). Tesla's technology has not only changed the world of automobiles, but it is also now proving it can accelerate the world's transition to sustainable energy.

+ *Uber*. Uber transformed the public access to transportation industry in a dramatic way. Many say it hurt the taxi industry, but it also spurred the creation of copycat companies like Lyft and helped foster the gig economy. In this case, Uber found a better way of serving the consumer, which in many cases forced the taxi business to make some dramatic changes to compete.

+ *Chick-Fil-A*. Chick-Fil-A has become a standout among its competitors in the fast-food chain industry in the past two decades. Most Americans used to have an image of hamburgers or pizza when thinking of a fast-food chain. Not anymore. Not only has Chik-Fil-A become one of the fastest growing fast-food chains in the world, but it has also done so without being open on Sundays like its competitors. Furthermore, they are competing in the standard "hamburger" space with brands such as McDonalds, Burger King, Wendy's, etc., without selling hamburgers. Its core product is breaded chicken, and their business model is 100 percent customer-experience based. Chick-Fil-A has rewritten the book on customer service and how to create a better customer experience, showing that it can be done differently.

+ *Airbnb*. Airbnb disrupted the hotel and vacation travel lodging industry. Their offerings range from rooms in private homes to entire houses for rent that are nicer, sometimes less expensive, and even located in out-of-the-way places where big chain hotels may not exist. Airbnb is also known for adding the personal touch of a local guide who gives tourists advice, sometimes offers transportation to and from airports, and provides other services hotels don't offer.

What are some things these industry disruptors and brand renegades have in common?

+ They have a true passion for their industry that drives a deep-seated need to succeed on their own terms.

+ They don't seek approval from anyone inside or outside the industry, which also means being tough enough to let criticism roll off their backs. Critics will speak loudly, and repeatedly. Note: This is not the same as refusing to seek input or advice from other experts. That is foolish. Any advice you choose to apply, however, must still fit your mentality and process plan.

+ They are willing to step way out of their comfort zone and re-create an existing business model.

+ They are unafraid to act, and if that action turns out to be a mistake, they don't wallow in fear or regret when making corrections.

+ They know how to take calculated risks based on the information available at that time.

+ They make affordable mistakes that won't cause the business to go under.

+ They have an in-depth connection to and understanding of their service or product that transcends "normal" business practices.

+ They see the big picture but act on what's in front of them at the moment.

Our Brand Renegade Journey

We are disruptors and renegades—in business in general and in the tattoo industry specifically. Ask some of the people we've pissed off over the past ten years, like the people who said we'd never make it if we changed this process or that system. Yet here we are!

Together we've created a multimillion-dollar company and have brought an industry perceived as dark, disreputable, and dirty more into the mainstream. We've cleaned it up, from the record keeping for tracking expenses and income to hiring and customer care, and from standardizing all systems and processes to expanding brand awareness.

Sean's key passion is for artistic creation and business acumen, and Thora's is for the business processes, studio design, and aesthetics. We both agree on our main goal: Together we will feature the art in a positive way, while caring for the employees and customers so the business can profit and we can give back to our community in bigger and better ways.

The success we've had can be duplicated in any industry because the keys to success, the tools to create change, and the attitudes required to maintain growth and momentum are the same across most businesses. We learned many lessons while on our mission to be the best we could be on our terms:

+ *Establish clear boundaries between business partners from the start.* This includes establishing who plays the role of bad guy and the good guy in different scenarios, from dealing with vendors, bankers, realtors, employees, customers, and others in every aspect of the business.

+ *Have a viable and equitable exit strategy in place from the start.* This is true whether you're a solopreneur or a partnership. It means having a Plan B in case of changes in market forces, personal circumstances, success that leads to a business sale, or the need to file for business bankruptcy.

+ *Learn and apply the difference between working ON the business vs. working IN the business.* Being hands-on rather than delegating can strangle your business. Knowing the difference and applying the different philosophies can also mean the difference between the business partners maintaining their sanity and long-term health, both individually and in relationship with each other.

+ *Understand the difference between being a leader and being a boss.* A boss talks down to employees and doesn't allow them the freedom and experience to grow to their full potential. A leader teaches employees how to do their job and encourages them to do so. A boss is often unforgiving when things don't go as planned, while a leader helps to brainstorm solutions and encourages employees to make adjustments and report back. A boss risks becoming a dictator who believes they know it all and it's "my way or the highway," as the old saying goes. A leader can become a teacher, explorer, confidant, and cheerleader.

+ *Find the balance between doing things out of passion and doing them out of necessity.* Let's face it, sometimes the things you have to do for your business to succeed just suck. Not every part of the job is something we look forward to doing. For example, hiring and firing employees can feel like one of the worst things you have to do. Rather than focusing on the negativity of letting someone go from your organization, use that energy instead to think about the upside potential you are bringing into your company by hiring someone with a new perspective and energy. Take these moments with a grain of salt and remind yourself that the fun parts of the job are still there.

+ *Develop short-term and long-term goals and readjust as needed, but don't half-ass it.* A lot of people who go into business just fly by the seat of their pants. Most decisions are made by reacting to events, rather than by proactively executing a plan. This business model kills decision making, or at least good decision making. It relies more on luck than skill, and luck can run out. You can keep improving your skills for the rest of your life.

+ *Trust external experts to supplement internal skills and services.* Learn from others, but don't necessarily do everything their way. For example, learn how to implement basic payroll or P&L software.

+ *Learn to take risks (some calculated and others not so much) and weigh the possible outcomes.* For example, a risk on locating your new business may take much more calculation and information gathering prior to the final decision vs. risking taking on a new vendor for fulfillment. Sometimes simple cost/quality analysis of competing vendors can be efficient enough to take a risk on changing your current operations.

+ *Don't trip over dollars to pick up pennies.* Evaluate which exercises are worth taking the time to do right vs. taking on everything and missing really valuable opportunities because you are too busy doing things that are not giving a return on your time invested.

Our goal is always to encourage new and existing business owners, business partners (spouses, family members, or friends who go into business together), and women in business to step up and do things that matter without fear or concern for what others think is possible for you and your business. This book is the story of how we made our opportunities to act, learn, and earn so we could give back to our community.

Yes, we made many mistakes, some smaller and some bigger, but all taught us valuable lessons. Yes, we saw huge losses at times, but we tried to take only risks that were recoverable, and not all our losses were financial. Yes, there are some things we would do differently if we could. Yes, there were tears and fears.

Yes, there were fights and disagreements, both professionally and personally. We have each matured and discovered more about our strengths and weaknesses.

Yes, we have learned a lot about general business, real estate, P&L, risk assessment, risk mitigation, debt, the IRS, state and local laws, leadership, friendship, family, and more.

And, yes, we will share many of our successes and failures and the stories that make them come to life, along with highlights and insights, with you.

CHAPTER

2

HARNESS THE POWER OF MENTORSHIP

When we look back and think of all the things we have been able to accomplish, it is honestly a bit of a surprise. One of the most common questions we get asked by other entrepreneurs is, "How did you do that?" No matter which achievement they're asking about, we seem to end up with the same answer most of the time. The common element is that we simply had the will to keep pushing forward, even when things got incredibly difficult or looked like they were about to fail.

How did we develop this determination? Were we born with it? Or is it something you can learn? We feel that the will and determination each of us has, along with the drive to continue working, were instilled in us at a young age. Our individual life circumstances contributed to that drive. But if you don't have the determination gene early on, that's OK. You can develop it as time goes on by encouraging yourself to meet goals that are important to you and practicing positive self-talk. Through the addition of solid habits, your determination and confidence will grow stronger. Determination means thinking, "I can, therefore, I will." Sometimes it is actually closer to "I must, therefore, I will." When failure is not an option, success is a foregone conclusion to those who can manifest it through sheer determination. This happens rarely, but it does happen.

These were and are useful tools; however, they became much more useful when we learned how to use them more efficiently through the guidance of our mentors. There are few more important ingredients in our success than our mentors. Without the people who helped guide us through that early uncertainty and fear, we would almost certainly have given up a long time ago. That is why we are so grateful to them, and why we try to mentor as many people as possible in our time. We feel that having mentors is an integral part of our success, which is why we want to dedicate an entire chapter to it: what they are, what they do, how to search for one, and, most important, why you need one. We'll also dive into what mentorship has meant to us and how you can make it a part of your own brand.

SEAN: *In my life, several people stand out to me as great mentors who went out of their way to give me advice and guide me when I needed it the most.*

My grandfather, Russell Walliser, is first on that list. He gave me assurance and guidance going back to when I was a young child in Phoenix. Grandpa Russ had a way of communicating that made sense, but he was strict enough to get after me when I was out of line.

He gave me belief in myself when I doubted my capabilities and pushed me to keep working at whatever it was I needed to do. Whether that meant tying a better knot in my fishing line or doing a better job on my homework or class project, he always seemed to give me the guidance and advice that I absolutely needed in order to move forward.

THORA: *I agree. The importance of finding a mentor who pushes you to be better cannot be overstated.*

As entrepreneurs, it is exciting to create something completely on your own. However, while you may have a great idea, you may not know how to develop it into a simple revenue generator or a sustainable business model. This is where mentors can be invaluable.

We have had several mentors over the years, and both of us have learned a tremendous number of valuable lessons from each of them. From avoiding poor business decisions to nurturing select partnerships, a mentor can help you navigate your entrepreneurial journey.

Whether you are starting a new business from the ground up or trying to develop new stages of growth for your company, a mentor can help guide you through any transitions you experience on the journey. This relationship does not have to be area specific. We have both had mentors that were not an expert in any one field per se, yet they had more life experience, and their guidance was invaluable.

Being a business owner can be an isolating experience. The long hours and self-containing environment that many business owners find themselves in can be a hurdle. We often do not have enough time to connect with our staff, friends, or perhaps other entrepreneurs who share the same problems and pain points. Entrepreneurs have many responsibilities to keep up with, but the most important part of our work is making time for our staff/employees so we can help them succeed, and in turn make our companies stronger.

We mentor small business owners and help them discover fascinating things about themselves and their own businesses. As mentors, we strive to be a constant presence in our mentees' lives. They need to know that they can count on us for solid advice.

As busy business owners, we know it is hard to dedicate the time needed to be a proper mentor. But it is equally (if not more) difficult for small business owners to admit that they need one. Sometimes their "can-do" attitude and sense of pride gets in the way of seeking out advice. The fear of looking foolish paralyzes many people into inaction and lack of pursuing a meaningful mentee relationship. We recognize this fear in many small business owners we work with and will sometimes ask questions to get our potential mentees to open up about their pain points.

When a true mentorship develops, the relationship is beneficial for both the mentor's and the mentee's personal and professional growth. Becoming mentors ourselves has helped us continue to learn, grow, and improve our practice each day.

In our mentor/mentee relationships, we think it is important to both that mentees bring their own unique skills, experiences, and knowledge to the relationship. Every one of us has something to teach other people, as well as many things we can learn from a mentorship.

WHAT IS A BUSINESS MENTOR?

A mentor won't be able to answer every question, but they can say or do the right things to motivate you into continuing to try. They will continually give you the reinforcement you need and push you when they sense you are about to give up. Any mentor will have an eagerness to share their failures, tips for success, and expertise.

A good mentor is always willing to share their knowledge and meet the mentee where they are currently in their development journey. A mentor will not take the mentoring relationship carelessly and understands that good mentoring requires time, patience, and commitment. They are also willing to share information and provide continued support to the mentee. Good mentors will reflect and share what it was like just starting out in their own business.

We have had a lot of people give us positive reinforcement over the years, but the people we truly feel grateful for are the ones who encouraged us to keep going when we felt like quitting. People like Kerry Rose, who gave Sean support and advice when we were opening the first Club Tattoo location in 1995. In addition, Sean's parents provided early mentorship by giving him an incredible work ethic and the understanding that you will only get back what you put into anything. Thora's mother contributed to her tireless determination and drive.

A good mentor gives the mentee an idea of what success in the field can look like. By showing the mentee what it takes to be productive and successful, they can model behaviors and actions that lead to success. They share the importance of having a positive attitude and act as a positive role model for their mentee.

Good business mentors do not take their responsibility casually. They are invested in the success of the mentee in the creation of their business or job. They also need to have strong communication skills. A good mentor is committed to helping their mentees find success and fulfillment in their industry. They share excitement and enthusiasm for a mentee's progress, which is empowering for the mentee in developing their own strengths, beliefs, and personal characteristics.

Mentors are able to illustrate how the business market is growing and changing while showing mentees how to pivot and grow.

They keep up with industry news by reading professional newsletters and magazines. They may even be thought leaders who contribute to industry-level publications. They are excited to share their knowledge with new people entering the field and take their role seriously in teaching their knowledge to others.

One of the key responsibilities of a good mentor is to provide guidance and constructive feedback to their mentee, which is an opportunity for the mentee to grow. By helping a mentee pinpoint their strengths and weaknesses, the mentor helps them see where they can improve attitudes and process to become more successful in their field. Adjusting communication styles to the personality style of the mentee helps facilitate these conversations.

Mentees want to look up to their mentors as people whom they can emulate in their own careers, possibly taking on the role of mentor for someone else one day. As such, they typically want to follow someone who is respected and whose opinion is valued by colleagues and employees.

Mentors value others and are willing to share the spotlight by empowering mentees through positive feedback and reinforcement. They are willing to listen to the differing opinions of others and come to collective conclusions on subjects they are not familiar with.

A mentor can make a real difference in your career and life. Come to the relationship with realistic expectations about the role and a willingness to work hard. The impact of a mentor's guidance and wisdom now may not be felt for some years to come, but you will realize its positive impact over time and go on to become a mentor to others.

Recently a business peer came by to talk and confided in us that they were experiencing challenges with their business partner's behaviors such as lack of honest communication, not showing up to work on time, and keeping up with his responsibilities of working in the business. We listened to him and shared that we had been in that same position more than once during our entrepreneurial careers. We advised him on how to approach his partner respectfully and communicate the issue in a way that might result in a positive outcome for both partners. We didn't take sides; we listened to their problem and sought the best way to get to the desired result, which was a better relationship between the two, so they could resume working on their very successful business.

WHY YOU SHOULD GET A MENTOR

Over the past 26 years in business, we have had a lot of experiences— some good, some not so good. There were days we left work feeling helpless, scared, hopeless, and alone. At times, we were embarrassed to confide in anyone that we were struggling, even each other (which was the absolute worst feeling).

Looking back, we are extraordinarily grateful for the people who helped us through those times, not because they were formal business mentors, but simply because they took the time to listen, care, and urge us to keep pushing forward. Through their impact on our lives, we learned the importance of being available to listen, support, and give critical feedback when needed.

We've created a list below of seven reasons why new business owners should seek out mentors—and why veteran business owners might want to take on a mentorship:

1. *Mentors are a plethora of information.* When we were starting out, we had no idea what was involved in running a business. If we would have had a mentor there in the beginning, we could have utilized a wealth of knowledge that may have helped us avoid costly mistakes. While we did have mentors growing up into our young adulthood, we had very few direct mentors when opening Club Tattoo.

   One that stands out to us was a man named Kerry Rose. Kerry managed Sean's band, Grey Daze, in the 1990s but also owned a restaurant called the Whale and Ale that Sean was a waiter at in 1995. During the entire process of developing the Club Tattoo business, Kerry gave Sean solid advice on business and most importantly helped him avoid a few critical mistakes such as negotiating a lease and budgeting for operating capital as well as employment insights.

2. *Mentors help you find improvement.* Mentors are really good at seeing what you cannot. The constructive criticism that our mentors offered us helped to do that. We appreciated that perspective and insight because we didn't want someone to give us a false sense of confidence when there might have been things easily improved upon had we simply known about them. We needed to identify exactly where we were falling short so we could improve those areas as quickly as possible.

3. *Mentors support personal and professional growth.* Our mentors would often ask questions for us to think about and ask us to come back with several different answers. They would also set various goals for us to see if we could accomplish them on our own. Our mentors made a point to tell us what they had observed throughout the process, what they thought

was worth doing, worth repeating—and what they might immediately get rid of.

4. *Mentors push you to do more.* A good mentor will be able to sense when you are struggling and can step in to offer positive encouragement. Mentors can help you identify fear and help you focus your energy into making proper decisions. There were times that, if there hadn't been a mentor for us, we could have easily given up emotionally, or given up on the business entirely. However, we had several along the way and each one wouldn't let us stop, instead they provided the encouragement and guidance that gave us the optimism, courage, and confidence that we could accomplish whatever we put our hearts, minds, and energy into.

Playing a dual role of coach and connector, a mentor (once they feel you are ready) may provide access to those within your industry that are willing to invest in your company, offer their skills and expertise, introduce you to talent that can fuel your business, and help you get closer to your target audience. Our mentors willingly shared their networks with us, sharing useful events and making introductions that led to many opportunities we would not have otherwise had. Most of the time the benefit was not monetary (i.e., investments) and was through introductions to people who could add value into what we were seeking.

5. *Mentors help us to see our limitations and work within them.* We have had many a tough conversation with our mentors as well, which usually resulted in us finally realizing a lesson they were trying to teach. They did this because they understood that being an entrepreneur, it can be difficult to find self-motivation and self-discipline. Our of our mentors, Wayne, took on the mentor role to teach us solid work habits and provided goals to focus on.

Owning a small business, it can be hard to know who to trust and whether you can trust someone, especially with proprietary information or intellectual property. Since Wayne was an objective third-party with no stake in any idea or venture, he was happy to let us know what he thought. In return, we knew that he would keep everything we told him confidential rather than sell it to someone else or take and use an idea from us.

6. *Mentors let us share ideas and give honest feedback.* When we started, we had ideas for all types of businesses. Our mentors were able to see what worked and what wouldn't for us. The honesty was often brutal, but incredibly useful. It was also nice to understand that it was more important for us to focus 100 percent in one area and make it great rather than be spread too thin, taking on multiple ideas of which none could get the proper attention and focus, thus, causing none of those ideas or business plans to develop into meaningful or successful actions.

7. *Mentors help prevent you from making easily identified mistakes.* A mentor has been where you are. They have made their own mistakes and are willing to share their battle stories so you don't end up doing the same thing. Starting a business is challenging enough, so if you can skip doing things the hard way, why wouldn't you?

   We are all about doing things better and more intelligently, so our mentors shared many stories about the mistakes they had made along their way that became solid learning lessons for us minus the pain and lost resources that come from making those mistakes.

We are fortunate enough to have had great mentors and are now in a position to return the favor to others who are getting their sea legs in the business world.

Many people attribute part of their professional growth to the guidance of a patient mentor who challenged them to think differently and open their eyes and mind to different perspectives. While each of us develops at our own pace, this type of influence can have many positive and long-term effects.

A mentor becomes a personal advocate for you, not so much in the public setting, but rather in your work life. Many organizations recognize the power of effective mentoring and have established programs to help younger professionals identify and gain support from a more experienced professional in this format. Here is what a mentor should do for you:

+ Help you see the long view of you and your brand's development.
+ Help you visualize your end game.
+ Help identify fear and encourage you to stay focused and make sound decisions.
+ Offer feedback and encouragement, but not dictate how you run your business.

Here is what a mentor should not do:

+ Constantly criticize without guidance.
+ Act like a boss to you.
+ Tell you how to do things.

YOUR JOB AS A MENTEE

When you find a mentor and establish a relationship, be sure to talk about what both parties expect to get from the relationship. Clearly identify how you will communicate, what's on and off the table for discussion, and what your goals are for the mentorship. Deadlines are a good way to follow up and respect each other's valuable time.

There is nothing more frustrating for a mentor than taking their valuable time and giving it to a mentee who does not take notes or apply the information given to them. Do not waste your mentor's time by being disrespectful of their input. This doesn't mean that you need to do everything that the mentor is suggesting; however, you should think about all of the information and support that your mentor provides and craft a meaningful response from your perspective using reason and logic.

Try to get as much as you can out of the mentor/mentee relationship while making sure your mentor feels heard and respected, too.

Think of ways that you can help to push and preserve your relationship with your mentor. While your mentor invests their time to help you, you must also participate and actively pursue learning.

Here are some steps to having a successful relationship with your mentor:

1. Take your time to research mentors before you connect with anyone.
2. Be vulnerable.
3. Don't expect your mentor to do the heavy lifting for you.
4. Do not expect mentors to have all the answers. Sometimes mentors will simply listen.
5. Be a good listener.
6. Offer feedback to your mentor. Let them know you value their advice.
7. Do not ask for or expect political/social/monetary favors or preferential treatment.

HOW TO LINK UP WITH MENTORS

There is a lot of knowledge and skill that can be shared between business owners in general. But how can we make the time to connect? In the year 2021 and beyond, technology can make a huge difference. There are several platforms that we have found to be specifically useful when it comes to connecting with potential mentors:

1. *Social media.* Social media platforms such as Facebook, LinkedIn, Instagram, and Twitter enable us to connect and share stories, ask questions, and interact in real time. These platforms offer small business owners a space to learn about issues they are facing and brainstorm ideas for making changes in their business or engage in conversations and promote some connections on their own. Many of these forums operate on Q&A engagement and are excellent resources.

2. *Books.* There are many books out there that will help you learn, many of which are shared on LinkedIn, Twitter, or Facebook, and are focused on whatever topic you might need to dive into for your business. Google is an enormous resource for finding content as well. Personally, we have read/ listened to (and continue to read/listen to) hundreds of books that have become large contributors to our professional and personal growth. Audiobooks are a great way to absorb new information and a super-efficient use of time in a car commute for daily driving. Sean averages a book a week simply by listening on his daily workout/run and daily commute. This is one of our top choices for continuing education for any small business owner.

3. *Clubs/social pages.* Another option for establishing mentorships that can be beneficial for small business owners is to create a group that centers mentoring and building leadership skills as its purpose. Facebook is an excellent resource for creating this. Sometimes we do not even realize that we are in a "mentorship relationship"; we are just supporting one another on our business journeys.

Experienced business owners need to seek out mentors as well, and that might mean connecting with a business owner who is new to your industry. They might not even be in your industry to develop a teaching/learning relationship. We have learned valuable lessons from farm owners and construction company entrepreneurs. If you are open to learning, you can take solid business principles from any industry and adapt and apply it to your business. Perspective and concepts can be applied and used in completely different arenas. In addition, there are literally hundreds of focused micro-communities available on Facebook and LinkedIn to connect based on subject matter and industry.

3

UNDERSTAND WHAT MAKES A PARTNER TICK

As you build your business and brand, you may opt to take on a partner. The success of your business ultimately rests on how well that partnership succeeds. And hopefully, what makes your partner tick is more akin to a stopwatch than a bomb!

Having a good partnership comes down to one thing: *not depending on your partner to make you happy*. Happiness comes from within yourself, and a great partnership is all about becoming a better partner, not *getting* a better partner. Understanding what your partner needs from you is an excellent way to create a successful relationship, whether that's in business or in your personal life.

We're not saying you should do everything for your partner. Far from it. Hold your partner accountable for their responsibilities in your business. However, by trying to be better yourself, your partner will hopefully take notice and do the same, resulting in a strong partnership that puts others before self.

THORA: *I find that when I put my partner first, Sean sees and appreciates my efforts that much more, and inevitably ends up working harder for our business because of it. Our biggest challenge early on was both of us failing to communicate; we were only able to overcome those issues by reflecting inward and doing better personally.*

In this chapter, we'll talk about why a strong partnership is so important for your growing business and brand. To do that, we're going to tell you the story of a partnership that went terribly wrong as well as one—ours—that went very right.

A CAUTIONARY TALE: SEAN'S LONG ROAD TO A SUCCESSFUL PARTNERSHIP

Through my teenage years and into my early 20s, I started several businesses, and because of this I have had many more business partnerships than Thora, so I will elaborate on several of them. I believe most people enter a partnership out of fear. They are scared to take on the risk of whatever business they're starting alone and believe that a partner may be able to do something better than they could. They may worry about not being able to work enough hours or not having the right people skills. The fear of not knowing all the answers—and, even worse, the fear of looking foolish for not knowing all the answers—can lead you into a partnership that does not serve your business well.

All these premises are, in truth, fallacies, that generally cause the partnership to fail much faster than the business itself. Yes, fear, is the ultimate motivator and consequently the root cause of most failures of partnerships. Most people don't realize that they may not even need a partner at all. I have had many partnerships over the years, and all but one were because I was afraid—the exception is my partnership with Thora.

Know Your "Why" . . . and Theirs

My first partnership was forming a band when I was 17 years old in 1990. It was called, embarrassingly enough, "Sean Dowdell and His Friends." It was my first band and my first attempt at a true business partnership. Of course, I did not know this at the time.

I thought of us as a band of brothers, and believed we had each other's back under any circumstances. That, of course, turned out to be false and preconceived with extremely unrealistic expectations based off the misguided premise that each one of us understood what the others wanted, what our individual goals were, and what each truly valued as humans, musicians, and band members. As time passed, I started to realize that each of us had a different "why." Of course, we all wanted to succeed, but each of us had different definitions of "success." Some of us wanted to rehearse and write music, some of us wanted to play live shows, and some of us just wanted to drink and party. We did manage to put together a three-song demo tape that got decent reviews and showed some promise. However, it was no surprise that the band disintegrated when we eventually found out that we were all on different pages.

In 1993, singer Chester Bennington and I went on to form another band (and partnership), Grey Daze.

Align Your Goals and Check Your Ego

My second partnership was far more successful than my first. I now had some experience and knew how to avoid some of the pitfalls—or so I thought. My new partners had a much more closely aligned mission, understood each other better, and had cohesive individual goals. We founded a group with a common goal between the partners. We were better communicators, and our work ethic was much stronger and closer in intensity.

We had many successes in this band, eventually signing three record contracts and putting out two albums together. Although we worked extremely hard, wrote great songs, and had a pretty solid future, this partnership eventually broke apart as well. Grey Daze played in front of thousands of people regularly and was getting radio play and national attention near the end of its first run (the band reunited in 2016 and released a new album in 2020 after Chester passed away).

But ultimately, the partnership fractured. The members had started to grow apart and discover conflicting individual goals. Some of them discovered drugs, and addiction is a recipe for disaster for any partnership. Some got married, and the four-way partnership we had in place became a five-way and eventually a six-way partnership, which necessarily introduced new opinions into the mix. This caused animosity, and eventually the band split in 1998.

Once again, I can look back now and see what caused the partnership to fail. We were not aligned in our collective vision, did not support one another's goals, and allowed resentment to build within the group. That resentment led to anger and eventually to arguments that would have been easily prevented if we had taken our egos out of the mix. Once arguments grow heated (at least for most young men), it becomes hard to let go of the anger, and it becomes a lasting grudge.

Avoid Complacency, Prioritize Communication, and Control Your Demons

During my time with Grey Daze, I also formed two other business partnerships. My third company was a live sound company called Antic-Round Sound with my friend Rick Snailum. We rented live audio equipment and provided sound engineering services to nightclubs and bands. That company lasted about 12 to 18 months (from 1993 to 1994). We were successful, but the work was time-consuming and laborious, and eventually we both lost interest and dissolved the business. It ended without animosity or resentment. We got along well, and Rick was a great guy, but our partnership didn't last because neither of us shared a passion for what we were doing.

In 1995, I entered my fourth partnership when I opened my first brick-and-mortar business in Tempe, Arizona, with my business partner and bandmate Mace Beyers. At this point, our music partnership in Grey Daze was going so well we decided to start another business together. We thought to ourselves, "Well, we are becoming successful in one partnership already—of course we will be successful in our second, and furthermore, it won't affect the other partnership/business we have together. We can keep it professional and separate."

Just to make sure we had our heads on straight, we decided to get advice from an attorney and have a partnership agreement drawn up. It was limited as to the inclusions, but this was a meaningful and helpful decision at the start of our company. The simple agreement outlined the basic expectations and responsibilities for each of us (or at least as much as we could conceive of at the time) and what to do in case the partnership went sideways and one or both partners wanted out.

But things did not exactly work out the way we had expected. Within three months of opening our business, Club Tattoo, we started having problems. Mace unfortunately had discovered drugs and alcohol and was headed down a very dark path. He would go missing for days without any communication, leaving me to do nearly all the work involved with building the new shop, and I began to resent him for it almost immediately. Thank God my friend and band member Chester ended up helping me instead.

Mace and I did not communicate very well. When I would try to bring up anything I was upset about, Mace would storm off or give me a litany of excuses as to why he could not hold up his end of the partnership. I probably could have dealt with most of these issues, at least for a while, but when I found Mace taking money from the business without telling me, I knew I could no longer be in business with him. (Back then, I did not realize it was Mace's addiction that was causing his behavior, and I wish I had known at the time.) Our partnership came to a swift end after six months.

In the first six months of any business, the financial burden and overall stress that is put on the owners of that business are immense, and without a good line of communication and expectations, the business is doomed to fail, let alone having one partner taking money from the company without the other's knowledge. This is exactly what happened to us.

Although our partnership ended, I went on to run Club Tattoo on my own. I bought Mace out of the partnership agreement in 1995, using our legally drafted agreement as a guideline, but I still had to remain partners with him in our band, which was thriving at the time. I had to walk a very thin line between what was fair and what would keep the peace and not cause lasting animosity but in the end our partnership failed due to addiction and lack of accountability.

While I was able to get him out of the partnership, the resentment did not go far.

Mace and I lasted in Grey Daze for another couple of years, but his drug addiction and alcoholism eventually took its toll, along with other factors. Chester went on to massive success in the band Linkin Park, which has sold more than 100 million albums and become one of the greatest-selling rock bands of all time. I was and still am immensely proud of everything that he accomplished with that band.

Grey Daze announced its reunion in 2016, when Chester and I created a video and released it on Instagram. It received nearly 3 million views, and the band started getting offers for touring around the world. We started recording a new album, but the process was cut short when Chester Bennington took his own life on July 20, 2017. We lost one of our best friends, an amazing business partner, and one hell of a great guy.

Watch for Early Signs of Trouble

In 1997, I was still in the band and had met my future wife, Thora; we were married the following year. She came from a business pedigree that I had never been around before and was very skilled at her career in marketing and sales, although she had shown little interest in becoming an entrepreneur. But in 1999, that all changed. She would eventually become not only my lifelong partner in marriage but also the best business partner I would ever have.

As I distanced myself from Grey Daze and formed a new band, I became extremely interested in the process of recording music.

I had been studying the various aspects of the recording industry for several years and had become fascinated with the technical side of recording music. So in 1999, I asked Thora and some mutual friends, Michael and Nancy, to form a new partnership and start a recording studio.

Once again, I knew we needed to have a well-thought-out plan, vision, goals, and expectations. I had learned from each of my previous businesses and was starting to have a better understanding of what made a solid partnership work. More important, I had learned what did *not* work in a partnership and had become better at predicting and avoiding these problems.

The four of us drew up formal partnership papers and went into business under the name SoundVision Recording Studios in November 1999. Despite our efforts at laying out everything in writing, we still noticed signs of trouble from our partners within a couple of months.

Originally, we had all agreed to contribute the recording equipment that Michael and I had both collected over the years. Thora and I owned ten times what Michael and Nancy did, but we did not care. We all wanted it to work, and if the business succeeded, it could buy the gear from us and make us even. In addition to the recording equipment, each party would invest $10,000 for the studio buildout (for a total of $20,000), and Michael and I would share labor equally in building it.

But within two weeks of signing our lease, Michael and Nancy admitted that they only had around $4,000 to invest. Thora and I were not happy to find ourselves stuck with a lease that we had personally guaranteed. If we had backed out, it would have been financially devastating to us.

Although our new partners had lied to us about how much they could afford to invest, and although it would dramatically limit the new business's resources, we decided to make up the shortage ourselves and try to make it work with our new partners. For what it's worth, Michael put in as many hours as I did on the initial build, helped get business into the studio, and was eager to learn.

I had much more experience than Michael when it came to engineering records and knew a lot more about the technical aspects of recording. I was willing to teach him what I knew and had him engineer most of the local bands that came into the studio. I was still playing with a new band called Waterface and had recently signed another record deal with Aezra/EMI Records. I was also working at Club Tattoo full time, so my time for running the newest business was limited. Michael was more than happy to learn on the job, and it provided much-needed income for his household. I only took on the larger bands that needed a more experienced engineer and helped Michael mix albums and finish off other projects.

Our recording business thrived even as our business relationship only limped along. SoundVision was making a profit, and we were reinvesting the money back into the business by buying new equipment almost every month. Things were going well, and everyone seemed to be happy. It was not the best partnership, but to be fair, we didn't argue much and we communicated better than most on important issues and goals.

Monitor Your Finances . . . Closely

In our third year of business, our lease was coming up for renewal. Michael had been pressing me to re-sign the lease, as he was now making a steady income at the business and had become a fairly good engineer with a lot of return clients. I initially had every intention of re-signing because we were turning a profit every month and I had a creative outlet through the recording studio.

I had taken a hands-off approach with SoundVision, producing only a few select projects. This meant that I was working there about 8 to 12 days a month, while Michael was producing about 15 to 20 days. He took the lion's share of work at the studio and was paid accordingly. I had no issues with it and neither did Thora. It seemed to be working out just fine.

One day I decided to take a look at the studio's finances to see if we could come to an understanding about paying us back for the initial overinvestment in equipment. I came into the studio one evening for the monotonous, time-consuming task of going through our financials.

While going through our bank statements, I came across a few checks made out to Michael that did not appear to be payroll checks and the amounts were too rounded to be supplies, compensations, or anything else I could think of at the time. Perplexed, I called Michael at home and told him I had been going through the bank statements and found several cashed checks for thousands of dollars made out to himself.

Michael got incredibly defensive and told me that Nancy had been fired from her job and his family needed the money to pay their mortgage and bills for several months. He basically said that the business had been doing well and the cash was in the bank, so he felt entitled to take it. He didn't see what the big deal was.

I not-so-calmly exclaimed, "If it wasn't such a big deal, then why didn't you tell Thora or myself?" Of course, he didn't have a reason. He half-assed apologized as soon as I told him I could not be his partner anymore. I think as soon as he realized he would no longer have a source of income, the panic started to set in.

Have an Exit Strategy and Know When to Activate It

It only took me a few minutes of thinking to get to a solid understanding of what Thora and I needed to do. After calling Thora and explaining what I had found, we knew we had to dissolve the partnership immediately. We could not be in business with someone who was stealing from the company, no matter what the reason was. We would have been understanding if Michael and Nancy had come to us and told us their financial situation, and probably even loaned them the money to get back on their feet until Nancy found a new job. But trying to hide it from us was a completely different story and very clearly let us know that our partners were dishonest and self-serving. In our experience, a partnership can survive many difficulties, but theft is an incurable problem that, like cancer, has to be cut out as soon as possible.

Everyone goes through tough times, but it is never an excuse to steal or lie to your partners. When times become rough is generally when you discover your or your partner's true character. That is when integrity shines the brightest—and, unfortunately, that's when you are most likely to find out that your image of yourself might not be a realistic one.

If you ever have a friend or a partner who is going through a truly difficult time, it is obviously important to try to help them, but you should also observe their character during this time. If they don't take shortcuts to get themselves out of it or hurt other people to benefit themselves, then make sure you keep those people in your life. An honest person with integrity is much harder to find in this world than most people think.

After speaking with Thora and pulling together a plan, I called Michael back and explained that we weren't as upset about the money as about the dishonesty. I told him we could no longer be partners and that I was going to liquidate the company assets immediately to pay off the remainder of the lease and close the studio's doors the following day. He put up a pretty good fight but was careful not to cross any lines, as he was still holding onto the hope that I would change my mind.

The next day I went to the bank and closed the account. I paid off all the outstanding lease payments and informed the landlord that we would be moving out in 30 days. I then rented a rental truck and went to the studio to start taking out the equipment. With Thora's help, I moved nearly all the recording equipment out the first day, and over the next three weeks, we sold it off on eBay for well over $100,000.

While I was incredibly upset at closing the studio, we now had a surplus of cash that we could invest into Club Tattoo. I had been wanting to expand the shop for quite some time but did not have the opportunity to do so until the neighboring tenant moved out in 2002. In hindsight, the timing could not have been better.

STARTING FRESH

We closed SoundVision in 2002. Thora had stopped working in her corporate career in 2000 after deciding that she wanted to become a massage therapist to help people with their pain. She enrolled in a top massage therapy college and dove headfirst into changing her career. During her time in school, she found out that she was pregnant with our second son. It was an amazing blessing for our family.

After graduating near the top of her class in 1999, Thora gave birth to our son Carston and was torn between being a full-time mother to our newest addition to the family and pursuing her new career in massage therapy. While Thora thoroughly enjoyed her work, she also wanted to spend more time with our newborn son. She ultimately realized that the massage industry was not as lucrative as she had hoped and saw massive opportunities in other areas. She was starting to get the entrepreneur itch.

We had several conversations after deciding to close the studio, and Thora continued to work as a therapist for several months. I finally saw an opportunity to expand Club Tattoo into the space next to our original location, which we had opened in 1995. I wanted to bring a retail space into the company and truly make it into something more than just a neighborhood tattoo shop.

Club Tattoo was truly becoming a brand, albeit a local one. We had tens of thousands of stickers all over the Phoenix metropolitan area, and we were becoming well-known for the quality and consistency of our work. I thought if we could continue to offer the best tattoo and piercing services to our clients while integrating fashion that complemented the lifestyle of our clients, we could significantly grow our brand. The problem was that I was not very fashionable, nor did I understand how to buy wholesale apparel.

After thinking about it, I went home to talk to Thora and pitched her on doubling the store's size in order to create and sell our own brand of apparel and complementary brands, to elevate Club Tattoo into what we wanted it to be. I wanted to bring her in as a partner because Thora had a great fashion sense, she knew what the public wanted, she had an amazing organizational mind, and she could help me bring Club Tattoo into a more modern era of doing business. Essentially, she could bring a desperately needed different perspective to a male-dominated industry.

I believe that lacking a foundation of solid communication, cohesive goals, and strategies to reach those goals were the biggest contributing causes to the failure of my previous partnerships. This is of course why most partnerships fail—lack of communication, accompanied by a lack of understanding and empathy. Instead, you need a willingness to sacrifice for the sake of benefiting your partner. If I was going to risk becoming business partners with my wife, I needed to massively change the way I had previously thought about partnerships. My other partnerships had failed, and I could not afford to lose my newest partner as well as my wife if things went badly this time. Unlike the fear that had pushed me to go into partnerships that were perhaps not ideal, this time fear was making me second-guess becoming business partners with my wife. This was uncharted territory for both of us.

It may seem like common sense now, but in the late 1990s and early 2000s, there was no such thing as a tattoo or piercing "brand." We were one of the first, and as a result, we made a lot of mistakes, but we also succeeded very quickly. This was partly due to our innovative thinking and implementation, but it was mostly because of our ability to work together and develop an extraordinarily strong partnership that has only grown over the many years we have been in business together.

Club Tattoo was already on its way to becoming successful before I became partners with Thora. But it never would have succeeded on such a grand scale without her.

OUR FORMULA FOR A SUCCESSFUL PARTNERSHIP

The success of our partnership is not predicated on us thinking exactly alike. It has evolved and grown stronger due to the different ways Thora and I think, the different approaches we take to solving problems, our ability to be freethinkers, and our ability to relinquish the leadership to each other in different situations. We are willing to share risks, responsibilities, and accountability.

In addition, we have learned to let each other do what we do best. This may sound simple, but I assure you it is not (at least, for us it was not!). Stepping aside and letting your partner do what they have in mind, when the leader in you wants to jump in and take over, is exceedingly difficult. Learning to trust your partner is an essential ingredient in a successful partnership. Stay in your lane and honor your partner's roles. Make sure they are well-defined, as are your roles, so that conflicts over boundaries are kept to a minimum.

Some of the keys to our partnership's strength are a willingness to work hard (which should be a given), to listen to each other, to seek out each other's advice and counsel, and to implement ideas that are not our own even when we disagree. Simply trying a different approach that a partner suggests can be valuable in strengthening your bond because it builds trust in your partner's willingness to try new ideas.

We don't have a "perfect partnership" (whatever that is), but we have been very successful in business together because of these factors and because of our willingness to sacrifice not only for each other but for the sake of the business as well. Putting your partner's needs in front of your own is a sign of maturity and can set you on the path to a great partnership. A true partnership is when your goal becomes not to find the perfect partner but to become a better partner.

IT'S YOUR CUSTOMER'S EXPERIENCE, NOT YOURS

Most small business owners know that they have a local presence in each market. However, the majority of small businesses fail to realize that no matter how small the business is, it is still a brand! It took us some time before we realized that we were much more than just a local business. We had a loyal following who would travel far distances to get to our stores. They didn't simply want a tattoo or piercing; they wanted the entire experience that our business gave them.

Generally speaking, people do not travel long distances for simple items, such as toilet paper or glue, that they do not want a customer experience for. They do, of course, make choices based on other criteria in their local community. If customers routinely travel past your competitors to get to your business, you have a brand that people are seeking.

They might be seeking an item you create, such as a pizza, clothing, or, in our case, a tattoo or piercing. They could be seeking the experience they receive within your company, even if you sell the exact same item they can purchase elsewhere. For example, at Nordstrom, the buyer can purchase almost everything in the store either online or at other retail outlets, but they most likely choose to shop there because of their customer experience. They could probably buy it at a retailer closer to them, maybe even cheaper, but they shop at Nordstrom because of the experience they get, such as the warranty or return policy, free gifts, or personal shopper assigned to them.

A customer's experience is often far more important than the actual product being sold, so you can create an extremely brand-loyal client from a great customer experience. Some clients are price-conscious only and will let the price of an item drive the purchasing power regardless of the quality of the experience. Take insurance, for example.

Any consumer can buy insurance at any time, and there is almost always an insurance company that can beat their current insurance costs. For some buyers, price is clearly the only factor that guides their purchasing decisions. But for other buyers, there is a different set of guidelines that they use to make their purchasing decisions. They want to "trust" the company insuring them and care about that more than cost. These buyers are thinking about what they are insuring and what will happen if the insurance actually needs to be used. For them, peace of mind, reputation, and trust are the factors that guide their buying decisions.

This second type of consumer was who we went after with Club Tattoo. We knew that we couldn't be—and honestly did not want to be—the cheapest, so we retargeted our approach to attract customers who needed to trust us with their tattoo or piercing, who believed that if there was a problem, we would make it right. It was the Club Tattoo experience that our clients craved as much as the actual tattoo or piercing. In this chapter, we'll discuss the various parts of the customer experience and how and why it's a vital part of your brand identity.

UNDERSTAND THE CUSTOMER'S JOURNEY

There are several typical customer experiences that can be a differentiating competitive advantage and give your company long-term market sustainability. For every step of the customer experience, you have an opportunity to either "please" or "attract" customers or uncover a pain point or negative experience for them that can be turned into a positive opportunity. "Customer journeys" have been around for years as helpful tools for business owners. Understanding the individual steps customers go through as they interact with your business will allow you to simplify or add value within a single step or across the entire journey.

Below are the three stages of every customer journey:

1. *Awareness.* During the awareness stage of the buyer's journey, your potential customers are just gaining awareness of what their problem is. They likely don't even know your brand yet. At this point, they are likely Googling and crowd-sourcing information on the issue they are looking to solve—not yet seeking a solution.

2. *Consideration.* When the buyer enters the consideration stage, they have identified their problem/issue and are looking for potential solutions online and with people they trust, often on social media. At this point, the buyer is ready to compare and contrast possible solutions.

3. *Decision.* The decision stage of the buyer's journey is all about assessing potential solutions and making a final call on a product or service. At this point, you are going head-to-head with your competitors, so this is where your marketing rubber meets the road.

Throughout the three stages of the customer's journey, there are several types of conscious actions your business can take in order to take advantage of the opportunity by creating a sale— and hopefully a long-term customer. Authors Nicolaj Siggelkow and Christian Terwiesch discuss these actions in their book, *Connected Strategy: Building Continuous Customer Relationships for Competitive Advantage* (Harvard Review Press, 2019). Here are some actions they note that we strive to take in our own business:

+ The *Respond-to-Desire* connected customer experience starts at the point in the journey when a customer knows precisely what they want. The company's goal is to make it as easy as possible for the customer to order, pay for, and receive the desired product in the desired quantity. Thus, respond-to-desire really softens the "respond" part of the customer journey.

+ The *Curated Suggestion* customer experience acts further upstream in the journey by helping the customer find the best possible option that would fulfill their needs; it helps with the request. Both Respond-to-Desire and Curated Suggestion experiences can work only if customers are aware of their needs or the business is intuitive enough to understand and translate their needs if they are unable to.

+ *Training/Coaching.* Behavior customer experiences help their customers at exactly that part of their journey: they raise consciousness of needs and push the customer into action, effectively helping with the recognize stage of the customer journey.

+ When the business becomes conscious of a customer's need even before the customer is aware of it, it is possible to create an *Automatic Execution* customer experience, in which your business solves the need of the customer proactively. In this case, the company can shorten the customer journey tremendously and increase the value to the customer. For example, companies that utilize a subscription-based purchasing model have this element deeply embedded into their own successful business models.

USE THE 4-R SYSTEM: RECOGNIZE, REQUEST, RESPOND, AND REPEAT

Even when your company can provide these customer experiences, there is another important ingredient for your company's long-term success. To truly create brand-aware customer relationships, you must be able to re-create these experiences. If a business can learn from repeated exchanges and experiences with customers, it can become better with the Recognize, Request, Respond, and Repeat system:

+ *Recognize* when an underlying need of the customer appears, and either the customer or the business is made aware of it.

+ *Request* when a need is converted into a request for a solution to the customer's particular need.

+ *Respond* when the customer receives and/or experiences a solution for their problem. Your business can reduce most conflicts within the customer journey by having a response to each of the three customer journey stages that resonates with the customer.

+ *Repeat* involves offering positive feedback consequences that eventually create vast, sustainable competitive advantages leading to long-term loyal customers who know, love, and seek out your brand.

In the ever-changing world of business, the focus is shifting from product- and location-based businesses to customer experience-based business models. Customers have more power than ever in their choices due to the growth and implementation of the internet into the consumer world. It is imperative that you recognize this shift and adjust your model accordingly.

Consumers want to be treated better to gain their loyalty. They want to know that their buying power matters to your company and that your business not only cares about their patronage but is willing to go after it by offering something above and beyond your competitors.

Companies that can create unique customer experiences can set themselves apart from the competition by using customer touchpoints, as you can see in Figure 4–1 on page 44.

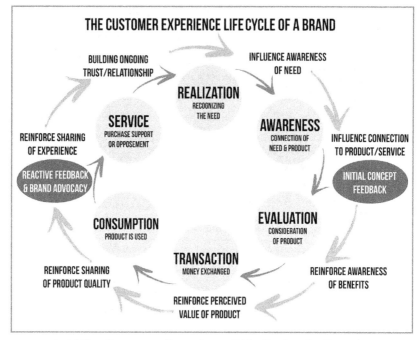

FIGURE **4–1** The Customer Experience Life Cycle of a Brand

Touchpoints are each stage in which a customer interacts with your brand. Every stage of interaction is a touchpoint, such as seeing an advertisement (realization and recognizing the need), standing in a store location, reading posts on social media (awareness and connection to product), calling the business to inquire about a product (evaluation and consideration of the product), and purchasing and using the product (consumption). Each stage is important and feeds into the next.

Before you can create this exceptional experience for your client, however, you must first recognize what your client cares about. As a business owner, you must understand that you're in the business of providing an experience, so how you make that happen is just as important as the product or service you sell.

What companies can you look at that have a great customer experience? The car company Tesla comes to mind for several reasons. It knows that to gain trust from its potential buyers, it must go above and beyond its competitors because it is creating a different customer experience than most consumers are used to for purchasing a vehicle. Tesla has created a differentiation simply by treating its clients differently. When a Tesla customer has a problem with one of its vehicles, they send a technician to the customer's location and either fix the vehicle on the spot or give the client a loaner vehicle until the repairs are done.

It is this mindset that gives Tesla a competitive advantage in the auto industry, and their competitors have started to take notice and make internal changes to their business model as well.

What experience can your company give your customers that will help identify and differentiate your brand? If you do not already know the answer, do the next easiest thing: ask your clients what they want.

Most of the time, your clients will be honest in telling you what they think of their customer experience and be willing to share ideas on how to improve it. Simply asking your customers' opinions can be a great way to connect with your clients and make their experience more personal. Be willing to go the extra mile and make your company stand out, but don't get caught up trying to match what your competitors are doing. Create your own unique client experience based on what you deem valuable based on your mission statement or goals—and, most important, what your customers respond to.

KEEP YOUR BRAND MESSAGING CONSISTENT

For your business to take hold within a given market, it must communicate a consistent message to its target audience over time. Many small businesses stumble by changing their marketing tools and messaging too often, which ends up confusing the potential customers. This doesn't give their potential customers a chance to digest their brand message or learn to instantly associate that brand with that specific product. Stay the course and remain consistent in your messaging.

Message consistency is imperative for customers to absorb your brand's uniqueness and character. This does not only apply to one form of your marketing. It needs to cross over multiple platforms, including social media, print ads, website, billboards, and even your business cards. It *all* must have a cohesive image and unified, coherent message, which will reinforce the dependability of your company, build trust from your clients, and eventually develop brand loyalty from the consumer.

A great example of consistent brand messaging is Nike, which has used the famous "swoosh" logo since 1971. It has almost not changed at all since its inception. In 1988 they added the slogan "Just Do It" to build an emotional connection with the consumer. They continue to use the swoosh and phrase to this day, and they have become synonymous with the brand.

The likelihood of your company ever becoming a brand titan like Nike is extremely small, but that doesn't mean we can't learn from their business modeling. There are certain processes and approaches that still pertain to small businesses. For Club Tattoo, we came up with several tag lines to accompany our logo that resonated with our clients. Two that stick out in our mind are "Join the Club" and "Art of Life." We still use the latter with our company logo to this day. You can see an example of how we incorporate this tag line in Figure 4–2 on page 47.

Don't mistake an icon or a logo for a brand. A logo or icon like the Nike swoosh is simply an identifying character for the brand. It is their "visual signature." Their logo symbolizes the values and qualities the consumer has already placed on the company Nike. For some, it may stand for high-quality sports gear, shoes, and clothing. But the inherent value of the symbol is in the branding that Nike has done over time through the quality of its products. It sometimes sends the message to its consumers through professional athletes, whom some of its customers aspire to be. Other ad campaigns tap into the "normal" or "above average" sports enthusiast, so certain consumers identify with them.

FIGURE **4–2** The Club Tattoo Logo

Your logo can be simple; it only needs to be an identifier for your clients, who know and understand your brand. Our logo is clean and sends a message of longevity, trust, and quality to those who know our brand and understand the values our company puts forward. Our tag lines add credence to our ad campaigns and appeal to the consumer who loves tattoos or piercings, but who is also willing to go out of their way and spend a little more for a better, longer-lasting product.

These are not earth-shattering ideals, but when our customers see the tag line "Join the Club," they feel like they are part of something cool by getting services through us, or feel as though they are about to join some exclusive club through the experience we offer. "Art of Life" takes a more esoteric approach, giving the customer a chance to apply the tag line to their everyday appreciation of art. When our clients feel like their tattoos are not only deeply meaningful to them, but considered a work of art, they more often than not want to share their art and experiences with others, both verbally and through social media. It has become a part of who they are and their lifestyle. Both work for different reasons and are used independently throughout our ad campaigns. Figure 4–3 on page 48 shows another

FIGURE **4–3** Another Club Tattoo Logo

use of our logo. This specific logo is meant for a more artistic visual interpretation of our brand, and still maintains our main branding but gives the end user (via merchandise such as T-shirt, glasses, or stickers) other options to buy and or represent.

What are you telling your clients with your business's marketing? Make sure the message is clear not only to you but also to the client who knows little or nothing about your business or brand. Do they understand the message you are trying to convey? What is your visual signature? If you do not know the answer, do some research and ask strangers to give feedback on your marketing materials. Ask them specifically what message they are receiving from your ads.

Is the messaging strong enough for clients to retain it and think of your brand when the need for your product arises? This can take time, but eventually, if your marketing strategy remains consistent and your messaging is powerful, then clients and even potential clients will come to think of your brand when the conversation turns to the type of product or service that you provide.

OFFER CONSISTENT CUSTOMER SERVICE

Many small businesses lose sight of who they are in their customers' eyes and fail to nourish that side of their company. Be deliberate in your approach to not only your marketing but also the everyday operations and expectations you put on yourself, your employees, and your customers.

First, let's answer the question "Why is it important to follow up with a customer?" It is imperative to follow up with customers for these five reasons:

1. Following up ensures your customer had a good experience and their expectations were met or exceeded on every touch-point.
2. It lets your customer know that you care, and it adds value to your brand perception.
3. It is a learning opportunity to find out what your brand identity is through the eyes of your clients.
4. It gives your brand a chance to repair anything that may have gone wrong at any of the touchpoints.
5. It builds and maintains the relationship between your client and your brand.

Following up with your customers makes them feel special and creates brand loyalty. Our company does a follow-up phone call with our customers to ask them how their experience in our studio went. If there is an issue, we do our absolute best to make it right. We even incentivize honest reviews and give out free stickers to make our clients feel they are truly part of the lifestyle brand of Club Tattoo. Following up is one of the attributes that separates us from our competitors.

How should your business train their staff in the art of customer follow-up? Here are some suggestions from *Business Insider* that we have adopted for our staff to use:

+ *Set expectations first.* If you do not set expectations, your customers will set their own. By being proactive, you can influence how they perceive their gratification with a definitive outcome.

+ *Follow up after the sale.* Businesses are usually great at getting the sale, but do not contact the customer until they want to make the next sale. This is also an opportunity to learn what your business could have done better during the customer's experience.

+ *Think ahead.* If there is a time of year or a product with which many customers experience difficulties, do not wait for them to call you. Get on the phone or email them at a minimum and get the dialogue going between your business and its customers.

+ *Remember (take notes).* Special anniversaries of customers doing business with your company or other milestones are a brilliant excuse to reach out to customers proactively.

+ *Make your client feel special.* Reach out with a special offer with no strings attached.

+ *Get personal.* People do business with those they know, like, and trust. If it fits your brand and business model, be more conversational in communicating.

+ *Empower your staff.* After appropriate training, give your employees the power to do what is best for customers in specific cases that fall outside normal guidelines. In our case, an example could be if we have a disgruntled client who was unhappy with a jewelry purchase. We have a store policy that explains to our customers that all jewelry sales are final and there are no refunds/returns for jewelry. However, we empowered our staff to make decisions to give a new piece of jewelry at no charge to certain clients, solely based on their understanding of the situation (if we gave them the wrong size, if the client had an irritation/reaction to the jewelry, etc.). This makes our staff feel in control and able to think on their feet in order to give a better experience to our clients, and they do not feel chained to a set of rules that have no room for interpretation through common sense or fairness. Helping your staff understand the importance of following up will be one of the biggest hurdles you will face. Create an action plan for following up with your customers and get your staff to buy into the importance of it. Eventually, it will become part of your company culture, and everyone's expectations will be harmonious and focused on the same outcome.

5

FROM SMALL BUSINESS TO BRAND

What makes you a brand? You might say it's your logo, or a specific product you sell, or your style. We think a brand includes all of the above, but most important, it is an identity that is shaped by the set of attributes your customers associate with your business. A "brand" is simply something that others recognize and may assign specific values to, by hearing or visualizing the word association, or by seeing the logo or detailed product.

Most people can identify brands that they either know about or use daily, such as Coke, Subway, Frosted Flakes, Mercedes-Benz, etc. Your business should have its own unique brand identity as well. To find out what your brand identity is, you need to ask yourself a few questions:

+ What does my company do or make?
+ What do my customers want?
+ What is our customers' experience?
+ Where does my company fit in its industry/market?
+ What is my niche?

In this chapter, we're going to cover what it truly means to be a brand so you can harness the power of your growing business and then scale it up like a brand renegade. Our goal is to help you find your niche and focus on what matters most—what you do well. Concentrate on what your business does best, improve upon that, and overcome the temptation of trying to be all things to all customers.

FIND YOUR NICHE—THEN DOUBLE DOWN

A *niche market* is commonly identified as a smaller category of a primary market for a specific product or service.

Take the retail coffee market. We are willing to bet that most consumers instantly think of Starbucks. Given that Starbucks is the best-known coffee brand in the world, would it ever make sense to compete with them head on? While these "mega brands" are known broadly, they also have a diverse set of niche (sub)markets within their core offering.

Most people might say they would never take on a large mega brand like Starbucks. However, there are plenty of entrepreneurs who believe different is good and bigger isn't always better. You might not want to become the largest coffee brand in the world, but maybe you're trying to open a small, dependable local coffee shop that caters to the local coffee connoisseurs.

Consider brands like Portland's Stumptown, which is more than willing to take on a brand like Starbucks. Not at the Starbucks game, of course; however, a smaller brand like Stumptown Coffee, can carve out a niche market for its specific target audience within that industry. Stumptown isn't interested in being the largest coffee company in the world. They are obsessed with producing the best coffee possible and attracting the highest-quality customers. The brand is an upscale, boutique coffeehouse for the discerning coffee connoisseur. More important, Stumptown customers live and breathe this concept and exercise their buying power accordingly.

Under this definition, ask yourself, "What would our product or service niche be?" What does our business do best, and how can that fit into a niche market in our industry? Pinpoint and focus on the one thing you do better than your competitors. Perfect it, call attention to it, and make it "your thing." One of the many items that make our company so different than most "tattoo parlors" is our customer service team that greets every client the moment they walk in the studio. The customer experience is set up from that moment on. Our environment is upscale, clean, and inviting to the consumer who wants a higher quality tattoo or piercing. This is atypical in the tattoo and piercing industry and sets us apart the moment the client walks into our business.

How can you make your product a differentiator within your industry? Define specifically how you can improve your processes or systems and help make your service or product delivery stand out from everyone else's. Do your homework and create a new form of delivery for your product or service. This differentiation will add to your unique brand identity.

When you develop a brand, you have created something more valuable than the product or service you sell. As a small business owner, you must find out what makes your brand special and highlight that. Is it truly your product? Is it the location of your business? Or is it the customer experience? Find it and capitalize on it to create long-term, loyal customers who will continue to seek out your brand.

LET GO OF ASSUMPTIONS AND RESET YOUR BRAND MINDSET

Small business owners make several common misguided assumptions about branding, including:

+ Small businesses do not have brand recognition.

+ My business is too small to be a brand.
+ There are so many competitors in our industry that striving for individuality is pointless.
+ Having the lowest price is the only thing that matters to my customers.

Do you recognize any of these assumptions in your own mindset? If so, your thought process may be a bit misguided. It took several years in business for us to start to recognize these limiting mindsets. We didn't realize that we could truly stand out as a national brand from other tattoo companies. We started out small but eventually realized that we could become a recognizable brand that people sought out based on how they related to us and not simply because we were the closest or cheapest. We knew that we had created something different within our industry when we realized that most of our clients were women.

We made a conscious choice when we opened Club Tattoo to disassociate ourselves from the stereotypical image of tattoo and piercing parlors as dark, dingy, and dirty. We didn't put up old, grubby, and outdated art on the walls, like most of our competitors at the time. We created a brightly lit interior with a roomy lobby and put the art designs into neat books that were laid out nicely onto our lobby tables. We were an upscale "studio" rather than a "parlor," and our clients could see we were different from the moment they walked in the door.

Do you feel that your company could benefit from branding itself differently? Before you dive into figuring out what your brand is, ask yourself what you want out of your brand. You should know the answers to the following questions so you can create a solid strategy that will help you achieve your desired outcome. So what's your goal? Ideally you might want all these things, but what is your priority? Pick one, start with a goal, and build a strategy to accomplish it. Do you want to:

+ Make more money?
+ Stand out from your competitors?

+ Be more consistent?
+ Be more effective?
+ Be better appreciated by your clients?
+ Make a difference in the world?

Many small businesses make the mistake of trying to please everyone. You can't, so stop trying. We had to come to this realization quite early when some clients would come in and expect us to price match with our competitors down the street. When we refused, we had angry customers on our hands. Nobody wants that, but we had to decide who our clients were going to be.

We chose to be an upscale experience, and we made it clear to our clients that we were not going to be the least expensive choice in the market, but we knew who our target audience was, and we had a fairly good idea of how to get in front of them. In the end, we helped our entire industry change their approach to business as a result.

DISCOVER AND DEFINE YOUR TARGET AUDIENCE

What and who is a target audience, and how do you find yours?

A target market/audience is a specific group of consumers that a business aims its marketing and advertising strategies at to sell a product or service. Defining your target market is the first step you should take when creating your marketing strategy. When selling any product or service, the first question you must ask yourself is, "Who is my target audience?" Knowing who you are trying to sell to is as important (or more important) as what you are selling. Figure 5–1 on page 58 gives you an idea of where to find your target audience, which is at the intersection of behaviors, demographics, interests, and location.

Before you can create marketing content that resonates with your potential customers, you must know who your intended audience is (as well as who they are not).

An audience definition should ideally connect these three core items:

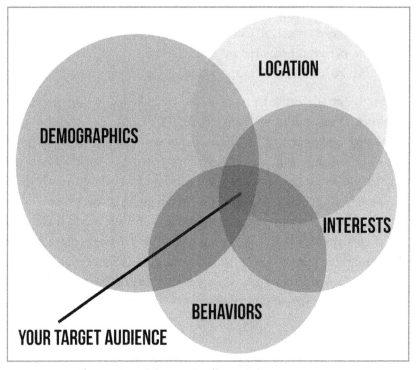

FIGURE **5-1** Where Your Target Audience Lives

+ Your product or service
+ The target audience's demographics
+ Your company's goal/mission

Do your research on your current customers, and create a system for collecting data on and tracking them. But you can't stop with collecting the data; you must then analyze and categorize it into a comprehensive and easily understandable database that will help you determine key details about your clients, including their age, location, and what they are likely to spend their money on.

As you capture this information, create a system to develop a client profile that is an overview of your clientele. The more you know about your customers, the easier it is to tailor your brand to them. Below are some examples of key identifiers you can use in developing your client profiles:

+ Gender
+ Age
+ Family lifestyle
+ Job function
+ Income
+ Location
+ Needs
+ Challenges

Many small businesses fall into the comfortable mindset of thinking they already know who their customers are. But without collecting and analyzing customer data, you are simply guessing, and that does your business a disservice. Do not **guess** at who your clients might be. Go through the focused exercise of finding out who they really are: where they live, how old they are, and what they want. We did an exercise to discover exactly who our core clients were at our original studio location in Tempe. We simply took a clip board and note pad and began asking each of our clients various demographic information such as age, sex, and where they lived. We thought most of our clients were college aged and approximately 50/50 women to men. To our surprise our age group was actually 24 to 32 and over 60 percent women. This was pretty easy to do, and once we did this for our companies, our bottom lines improved dramatically. We could identify the items that we needed to sell, such as more of our fancy navel and ornate nostril jewelry (an item that was 99 percent sold to our female clientele)—and more important, the items our clients wanted to buy—much easier and stopped wasting money on guessing.

LEVERAGE YOUR BRAND BY APPEALING TO EMOTION

We ended up saving a tremendous amount of time and money because we finally knew who we were selling to and why. Once you identify exactly who your clients are, specifically targeting those customers becomes much easier, and you can determine which marketing tactics and styles are best for your company. One such tactic that has been extremely successful for us is the use of emotional appeal. We created an ad campaign that showed a portrait tattoo of a woman's mother. The story behind this client's tattoo was that she had lost her mother to cancer a few weeks prior and wanted to get a memorial tattoo in honor of her mother. Simply showing the photo of the daughter with her mom's portrait on her arm appealed to the emotional content of the tattoo. We had hoped that potential clients might see this and think about getting something that touched them emotionally tattooed on their body.

Emotional branding refers to the practice of building brands that appeal directly to a consumers emotions. This directly correlates to the "Respond" stage of the customer journey (which you read about in Chapter 4). The company leverages the emotions of the potential customer and specifically designs its marketing to appeal to those emotions so the customers will purchase its product.

When you can define the key requirements and problems of your target audience, it is easier to design a marketing appeal that shows how your brand can help them achieve their desired emotional state by purchasing your product.

One great example of how brands use this appeal is Coca-Cola. Coke has long sought to tap into the emotion of happiness and fun with its brand messaging strategy, connecting its product with people having a great time. Whether the actual customer will ever do the activity being shown isn't the point. Coke is selling the idea that, if you drink Coca-Cola, you are part of the group of people having fun. Customers can be conditioned to buy based on this association.

Another example is Kay Jewelers' "Every kiss begins with Kay" marketing slogan, which correlates buying their jewelry with the amount of love you feel for your partner or other loved one. The consumer is conditioned over time to buy more, based on the assumption that the more they spend, the more they must love their partner. It sounds ludicrous, but it also works.

Don't be afraid to use the emotional connections your clients may have with your product or service to your advantage, as long as you approach it ethically. There are companies that use the emotion of fear to sell, and this is one technique we are adamantly opposed to. In our businesses, we focus on positive emotions rather than using fear as a motivator to get our customers to purchase something. We find ways to make our clients feel good about themselves and make their purchasing decisions from that state of mind. One specific ad campaign that we ran focused on "feeling good about looking good" and showed the quality of our tattoo artists and our jewelry. Our ad showed a couple smiling and enjoying a night on the town while proudly showing off the woman's beautiful back tattoo in a dress.

The ad focused on people having fun and feeling confident about the way they looked, and a part of how they looked was the quality of their tattoos and body jewelry. Many women feel good about having a nice, branded handbag, and tattoos are very similar in that other people notice the quality of what you have.

APPEAL TO CUSTOMER VALUES

Never underestimate the importance of adding value to the experience of your customers or potential business partners. Value in this context means:

$$\text{(actual value customers receive)} =$$
$$\text{(benefits of a product or service)} - \text{costs}$$

There are several factors involved in creating a value proposition for your potential clients. Note that there are many things other than price that customers deem valuable. In fact, price commonly ranks last when determining value. Different customers will have different ideas about what they value and how they want your brand to answer to those values. There may also be a product attribute that customers may feel is more important over a competitive product that is only sold at one business location.

Your customers keep your brand alive and well. How they view your brand is how others will, too. So, you need to understand what their values are in order to reflect it in your brand more broadly. Take every opportunity you can to capture customer data so you can keep on top of who they are and what they want. Create a survey that is specifically targeted to your customers and whatever you sell. Do not ask them leading questions; the goal is to get honest answers so you can adjust your business accordingly.

Understand your unique value proposition and be able to share that with customers to they can see the connection between your values and what you offer to them. This is where you can find and promote your niche within your industry to set yourself apart from the competition.

Create a competitive price, although not necessarily the cheapest price (unless that is your business model's biggest strength). Set your prices so customers can see that they are getting good value—but don't price yourself out of your market. Customers who value your brand will be willing to pay more over time once they receive the value you promise.

Avoid setting up your prices to reflect a fixed amount of product costs. Doing so tends to mean that you will end up giving away margin. In our companies, we never tried to be the cheapest in the market. We felt like that was a race to the bottom that always ended up lowering the quality of the product.

Instead of worrying about how much money you will make for a specific business opportunity (a mistake many small business owners make), you should focus on creating value; the monetary reward will come in time. Learn to maximize your unique position offering to its fullest advantage.

We would rather create a valuable position, partnership, or experience first and *then* worry about the financial gain. That way we know we did our best on the front end, leaving nothing else that "could have" been done. In our experience, this approach has almost always paid dividends, either immediately or further down the road when another opportunity comes along because of the value we added in the previous transaction.

CHAPTER

6

MARKETING . . . WHERE DO WE BEGIN?

Most small business owners will tell you it's not easy to compete with a global brand, and they're right. It is nearly impossible to compete with the likes of Nike, Sony, Disney, or Pizza Hut. So how do you approach a situation like this as a brand renegade? How *does* David beat Goliath?

You might want to start by thinking smaller. That's right—smaller.

Remember that in most small businesses you are realistically competing only for a small group of potential customers. Your target audience, for the most part, is in a limited demographic defined by geographic area, gender, age range, and many other characteristics.

Understanding what your brand is and who your clients are comes first, but it is also imperative to understand your business's place within your community. You need to know where your customers live, how many will potentially come into your business to spend money, and what motivates their buying habits. These are the attributes that will let you compete with the giant companies—or, at minimum, be able to flourish in your specific market. In this chapter, we'll show you why you need a strong marketing strategy to ramp up your brand and gain a unique market identity.

THE FOUR KEYS TO MARKETING SUCCESS

If you own a small business and are constantly thinking about how to compete with the big players, there are several factors you need to understand *before* you develop your marketing strategy:

+ Who are your customers (age, gender, proximity, etc.)?
+ What do they buy and how often (daily, weekly, monthly, yearly)?
+ Does your company have a differentiating factor over its competitors?
+ What is it, and how can you implement that into a key marketing focus?
+ What is the most cost-efficient way to reach your/their clients?
+ What is the CAC (Customer Acquisition Cost) to convert their customers into yours, and is it possible (over what timeline)?

Once you have answered these questions, you need to create and implement a strategy for your company's marketing. We have come up with four keys to developing a successful initial marketing strategy, and we will share examples of how we use each within our companies. You can succeed if you only focus on some of these keys; however, if you can pay attention to all of them, your company will be stronger and more viable in today's marketplace. Keep in mind, we use these keys for specific purposes in our own business model, so adapt them accordingly:

1. Determine your product or service
2. Pinpoint your target market
3. Understand your competition
4. Identify your niche

Let's look at each in turn.

DETERMINE YOUR PRODUCT OR SERVICE

Think about how your product or service looks and is presented. Does it reflect your customers' expectations?

We started out advertising Club Tattoo with hand-drawn fliers and posters, but by far our most successful promotional tool was our stickers. In the music scene in the 1990s, it was popular for young people to have a sticker of their favorite band on their car, so we made similar stickers for Club Tattoo. The idea took off right away, and Club Tattoo stickers started popping up all over the Phoenix metropolitan valley.

However, we wanted to differentiate Club Tattoo from our competitors even in something as minor as stickers. We didn't just buy a generic rectangular sticker, instead going with one that was much more expensive: $1.50 each for the smaller ones at 8-by-2 inches, which showed the shop's logo, or a whopping $5 each for the 36-by-4 inch die-cut stickers in the logo of "Club Tattoo."

One advantage of our stickers was that they had a degree of ambiguity as well as positive branding. Someone who might not have ever heard of Club Tattoo could see one of our stickers and think, "I have a tattoo; I want to be part of the 'club'; I want one of those stickers." It gave the feeling of inclusivity to people, and before long we had people coming into the shop just for a sticker because they loved the way it looked on their car and it made them feel like they belonged to the tattoo community.

Another way we differentiated ourselves was by giving the stickers away for free. It was a huge expense at the time, but we calculated that people driving around with our brand on their cars was basically free advertising for us. We wrote it off as a marketing expense and—wow, did it pay off for us. By 2020, we had given out more than 450,000 Club Tattoo stickers in many colors, sizes, and variations, and through tracking how customers were finding us, we calculated that it accounted for about 20 percent of our new business!

The stickers became such an enormous part of our marketing that eventually we started holding contests for people to take photos of where they posted their Club Tattoo sticker. The top prize was $500, and we got hundreds of entries each year. This created a local buzz and generated business, all in the name of promoting our brand.

Our personal favorite entry was one of the very first contest winners, an entry photo that came in from an American soldier who was deployed on his first tour in Iraq in 2003. The U.S. soldiers were tasked with taking down and destroying all the Saddam Hussein billboards, signs, and other propaganda across the country, and this Club Tattoo client and fan did just that, as you can see in Figure 6–1. He and his team tore down this billboard, put his Club Tattoo sticker

FIGURE 6-1 Winning 2002/2003 Sticker Contest Entry from Soldier in Iraq War

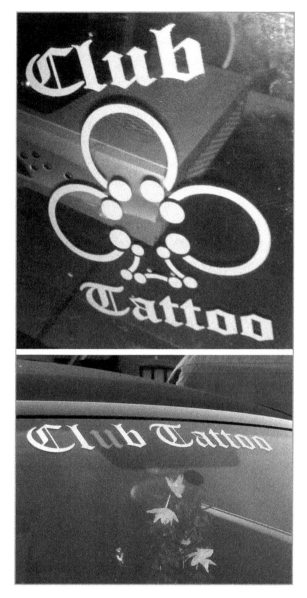

FIGURE **6-2** Examples of Club Tattoo Stickers

on it, and snapped this photo. Figure 6–2 shows other examples of other contest entries and clients that proudly display our stickers.

PINPOINT YOUR TARGET MARKET

You never know who could be a potential client for your product. But let's get real—you probably don't have the time or money to advertise to everyone. Instead, think about who your perfect customer might be. *That is the person you should target your marketing time and treasure to. Think about the demographics at play like age, interests, income, gender, needs, etc. Then you can build your outreach.*

It took several years for us to pinpoint exactly who our clients were demographically, simply due to our failure to collect accurate data. Or, to be honest, we were capturing the data, but we weren't analyzing what it meant or fully understanding why it was important. We thought we knew who our clients were until we started gathering personal information from them at our point-of-sale register. We did this in six of our studios over a period of 60 days to capture a snapshot of what was happening. Once we had gathered and analyzed the data, we found that our strongest customer sector (approximately 50 percent of our clientele) were women, with an average age of 28, who lived within a three-mile radius of each location, and made $40,000 to $70,000 per year.

With this vital information, we finally understood how to identify and reach our target market. We implemented a monthly email marketing campaign via Constant Contact and sent out different information to our clients based on the time of year and which customers we were trying to attract with a certain promotion. Knowing who our clients were meant we could push certain products to specific customers, and for a few dollars a month we could see how many actually opened the email, who read it, and who clicked through its options. With this much data coming in, it was painless to send the clients who interacted with our email newsletters promotions tailored to their interests. After implementing this system, we saw an instant response from the recipients, and our online sales grew over 50 percent in two months.

UNDERSTAND YOUR COMPETITION

Even if you aren't aware of any direct competitors, there is always competition of some kind—even if that means you are competing against outside factors like trends or world events. There is always going to be something or someone competing for your target market's money.

What can you do to control your competition? The answer is nothing. All you can do is control how YOU react to what the other guy is doing—and do it better. In other words, you still have to *understand* the competition. It is important to know roughly what your competition's business practices are and what they're selling in terms of brands or styles. But it's equally important not to obsess about what your competition is doing. That can drive some people to lose focus on their own company. Remember, every second you spend worrying about what your competition is doing is one less second you are spending on improving your company and moving forward with your business.

Find out what makes you different from your competitors, and focus on the positive attributes of your company by making sure your customers know what those differences are. Do something positive with that pent-up energy and befriend your competitors. A positive professional relationship with them will hopefully get them to react with a constructive attitude toward your company.

When faced with a problem like your staff leaving or a competitor spreading rumors about your company, again, the answer is to do nothing. Let your competition think they are hurting you. Let them obsess over what you are doing, not the other way around. Let employees who want to work elsewhere go. You can't have a successful working relationship with people who don't want to be there. In the end, it only matters what you are doing to make your business better.

Club Tattoo has grown almost every year we have been in business (more than 26 years at the time of writing this book). There have only been two exceptions. The first was the 2008 economic crisis, when most retailers and commercial businesses saw some decrease in revenues the following year. Although at the time it felt like a very large hit to our income, and we were tremendously worried about the long-term impact of the recession, it amounted to a modest 7 percent decrease from the previous year overall.

The second occurred (or I should say "is occurring" as we write this book) during the Covid-19 outbreak of 2020 (see Chapter 15 for more on this). It remains to be seen how large an impact this will have on our company; it will certainly be much more significant than the 2008 downturn. However, we are confident in our short-term and long-term strategies and feel that our businesses will not just survive the pandemic but will most likely come out of it stronger than before.

IDENTIFY YOUR NICHE

We talked about leaning into a niche in Chapter 5, but it bears repeating in terms of using various marketing approaches for your brand. Ask yourself: Is there a target market that perhaps you are not currently serving or that could use more attention?

While trying to define our niche, we had to decide what it was about Club Tattoo that was different from all the other local tattoo and piercing studios. It was easy in 1995, because there were only ten other tattoo and piercing shops in the entire state of Arizona (as opposed to over 350 in 2021). With that little competition, it was easy to stand out, but we still had to define what our specific appeal was. We started to market our higher-quality tattoos through channels such as full-color fliers (although it is commonplace now, believe it or not this was a huge luxury in the late 1990s) and through local TV commercials. These marketing techniques alone set us apart because they took a much higher front-end investment and visibly took on a higher-quality presence of their own. We made a point to specifically not apologize for our higher prices and explained that you get what you were paying for with our company. We started to get a more well-defined clientele. Eventually the low-price shoppers stopped coming around as our reputation for being a higher-quality and higher-priced company started to get noticed.

As time went on, we understood we had to provide a high-quality tattoo or piercing, but we also knew that there was an untapped market for an upscale *experience* for our clients. This had never been done in the industry, and we would have to figure it out as we went. It certainly did not happen overnight.

One of the first changes we made was to offer private rooms for our tattooing and piercing services. In the 1990s, most tattoo studios consisted of an open room, with four or five artists all working together. That left the clients completely exposed, whether they liked it or not. By providing private rooms, Club Tattoo became unique: now customers could get a tattoo or piercing without strangers watching them do it.

More recently, especially with the advent of social media, it has become more popular for clients to want to be seen as they are getting tattooed or pierced, since it has become common to take selfies and show the world what you are doing at any given moment. We still offer our private rooms for those who want them, and now we can accommodate everyone.

Another easy way to create a brand niche was pricing. We quickly—and intentionally—became known as one of the more expensive studios in the country. A product or service's perceived value matters. There is an ample supply of clients who want to pay a higher price for a tattoo or piercing, knowing that not only are they receiving a higher-quality product but also that they are getting it from a business with a higher perceived social status, in much the same way as shoppers at Neiman Marcus or Saks Fifth Avenue perceive their purchases. Those who want the best will seek out the best and are willing to pay a higher price for it.

But in order to be the best, you must be known and perceived as the best within your market. Our higher prices came with a quality that our competitors could not or did not want to provide. First and foremost, we went after and hired the best tattoo artists and body piercers available and paid them accordingly. We put forward a creative environment that the artists could thrive and grow in, but also put in place a professional atmosphere that was quite different from the industry norm that had its own appeal to those wanting a long-term career that was considered better than what the competition could offer. We had to be able to put out the highest-quality tattoos and piercings, or everything would be for nothing.

We invested in the most expensive sterilizers on the market and initiated monthly spore testing for each studio, proudly displaying the results. In addition, we created a set of cleaning standards that was put on display for our clients. They would watch as the artist and/or piercer would tear open their sterilized instruments and showed off the single-use items that were to be used for their, and only their, procedures. It gave them a deeper understanding of how seriously we took their health and safety, but also gave an underlying reason to justify our price points. We use only the highest implant-grade manufacturers of body jewelry, with an emphasis on American-made products. Our customers understood very quickly that there was a good reason we charged more, and it was simply because we were giving them more in terms of safety and value.

If customers want to buy high-quality gold and diamond earrings, rings, or necklaces, they can find those at Neiman Marcus; however, the niche created by our industry has left a gap we stepped up to fill, offering high-end gold, platinum, and diamond body jewelry along with the more standard varieties.

But simply selling expensive body jewelry is not enough; it needs to come with a high level of expertise from a body piercer who understands human anatomy and can place the jewelry correctly, or at minimum help the client select the proper piece of jewelry for their piercing. Some of these larger retailers who want to offer body jewelry have started to partner with companies like Club Tattoo to do small retail implant pop-ups to provide more value to their customers. Smart companies won't be left on the sidelines for long; they will find a way to participate. When we have done these pop-ups in the past, they have gone very well. In the future we will only participate in pop-up events if the event is a co-branding opportunity and not simply being paid to tattoo or pierce in someone else's branded environment. There must be an upside for our company's exposure, branding, and so on other than money for us to participate. Collaborative branding opportunities are great if they benefit both companies.

ONLINE REVIEWS

In a time when customers scavenge the internet in search of the best deals, greatest values, and newest trends, one of the biggest factors that has helped our company succeed is positive online reviews. Most customers will have a preconceived notion of what kind of experience they will have before they ever do business with you. Have you ever been in a conversation with friends when someone brings up a local restaurant and someone else says, "Oh, that place is awful"? Later on you discover they haven't actually eaten there; they just read a review on Yelp or saw someone's post on Twitter.

This is a human reaction: they want to be "in the know," so they will swear a place is terrible based on other people's experiences. As a business owner, you must stay ahead of this curve. Ask your customers to go online and leave reviews of your business. Make sure they are honest, as people will see through falsely placed and biased reviews. Positive reviews will make your business stand out from your competitors and drive traffic to you at literally no cost.

In the event of receiving a negative review, there are several ways to approach how you react. The first thing we prefer is to reach out to the client ASAP and find out if there is a way we can fix their bad experience. This may come with an offer to replace a piece of jewelry or touch up a tattoo at no cost. The key is to make sure the client feels like you have heard them and understand why they are upset. Usually if the client feels like they are being listened to, then they are more likely to return to your business and give you a chance to redeem their review and overall opinion of your company. It is especially important to try to get a second chance with your customer and fix the issue if at all possible.

Of course, sometimes the customer is not always right and simply will leave a negative review to try to get something for free. We have experienced this a few times, and, in this case, we try to accommodate the client at first, but if the request goes too far or will cost the company too much money, we may refuse the request. Although this is rare, it does happen, and we have standards to abide by and hold ourselves too as well. The best way to defeat the negative reviews is to simply drown them out with an overwhelming number of positive reviews that describe a personal experience other readers will connect with.

7

KEEP IT UP . . . IT'S WORKING

Once your company has put into place the basic components of an initial marketing strategy, it is time to analyze what you have done, find out whether your brand marketing plan is working, and refine and adjust those components. Far too often, we spent unnecessary money by believing the metrics of the person or company selling an advertising plan to us, rather than looking at our internal analytics to see whether our ad dollars were giving us a reasonable return on our investment.

It is imperative to know what you are doing to market your company, why you are doing it, and whether it is working. When reviewing your marketing costs, knowing what to stop spending your money on is just as important as continuing to spend on what is working. Many times, we spent money on things we assumed were working. Had we done our research in a timely manner, we would have saved ourselves much effort and cash. In this chapter, we'll walk you through four ways to measure your marketing impact and brand effectiveness that we still use and measure to this day: encourage brand awareness, build brand integrity, be dependable, and focus your brand marketing. Let's look at each of them in turn.

ENCOURAGE BRAND AWARENESS

Potential clients won't buy your product or service if they don't know the brand. Most prospective customers have to be exposed to your product several times before they think about making a purchase. So, it's important that you stay in front of your clients on a consistent basis.

One of the biggest and earliest marketing tactics we used at Club Tattoo was taken from Sean's experiences in Grey Daze, when the band would promote its live concerts by plastering the city in stickers, fliers, and anything else it could put its name on. Grey Daze were masters of creating "brand awareness," at least on the local level, and in the mid- to late 1990s, we tailored those guerrilla marketing techniques to Club Tattoo. In 1995 to 1996, we started producing a simple sticker for vehicles that within months was popping up everywhere in the greater Phoenix area. This sticker (which you read about in Chapter 6) continued to serve our branding efforts well for the next 25 years.

BUILD BRAND INTEGRITY

While it's vital that potential clients are aware of your product or service, that alone isn't enough to achieve brand awareness and secure repeat customers. The trust you build between your brand and your customers is one of the most important elements of your brand and business. The trust isn't free, though. To get (and keep) it, you have to come through on your brand's promise, allow customers to try out the product or get a closer look at it in action, and deliver a satisfying experience each and every time. There are many different ways to achieve this kind of integrity. We chose to give some of our products and services away to what would today be called "key influencers": we sought out good-looking bartenders, waitresses, and waiters at the local clubs who seemed to have a following and offered to give them a free tattoo or piercing if they would let all their clients and co-workers know how great their experience was with Club Tattoo. These were the social influencers who helped us build our brand by sending all of their clients to us and raving about their experience with us.

Today this type of campaign is even easier because local influencers in 2021 can reach their followers through social media. We can easily find someone with 100,000-plus followers on Instagram, Facebook, TikTok, or Twitter and track their followers to see if they fall within a reasonable radius of our business locations. If the influencer has the potential to reach our target market, we can reach out to them and see if they want to come in and get a tattoo, piercing, or jewelry upgrade. These types of influencers can have an instant impact on your business. They are not quite celebrities, but they can bring potential clients to your business just by endorsing your product or service. Don't blindly chase an influencer just because they have a lot of followers. Do the research and see if they are a good brand fit for your customers.

One possibility, which can require genuine luck, is getting support for your brand from actual celebrities. This is generally not something you can control, but you must make sure that if a celebrity does come into your store, you capture the moment.

We have been blessed by Chester and Sean being in the music industry and having many connections with celebrities. They could bring stars like Blake Shelton, Miranda Lambert, and Miley Cyrus into the studio to get tattooed or pierced. Figure 7–1 on page 78 shows just a few of the famous faces we've seen at Club Tattoo.

Over the years we have tattooed or pierced hundreds of actors, musicians, rappers, and professional sports figures, including musician DJ Steve Aoki, NFL player Vernon Davis, celebrity chef Guy Fieri, actor Don Gibb, Great White, Guns N' Roses, actor Jonah

FIGURE **7-1** Club Tattoo's Clients Include (left to right) Blake Shelton, Slash, Frank Mir, Chester Bennington, and Ewan McGregor

Hill, Korn, singer Miranda Lambert, actor Ewan McGregor, actor Chrissy Metz, UFC champion Frank Mir, musician Vinnie Paul, actor Teri Polo, MLB players Héctor Sánchez and Pablo Sandoval, musician Slash, Slayer, actor Brenda Song, actor Tori Spelling, Stone Temple Pilots, NBA player Amar'e Stoudemire, NFL player Terrell Suggs, pro wrestler Jack Swagger, UFC Hall of Famer Frank Trigg, musician Yandel, and hundreds more.

It seemed as if once one celebrity came in to get tattooed (and we let the world know about it), other celebrities wanted to get work done as well. It was a giant snowball effect that has helped boost Club Tattoo's worldwide image tremendously.

Of course, if you aren't fortunate enough to get celebrity endorsements, nothing helps your brand more than free press. We started with approaching some of the local magazines, which simply needed content to fill their pages, and asked them to write a feature story on Club Tattoo. Many turned us down, but it only takes one to get the ball rolling, and then you can build off that. By 2021 we had more than 300 articles written on us, our brand, and our business, as well as its impact on the tattoo and piercing industry, in such publications as *Entrepreneur* magazine, *GQ*, *Success*, *Rolling Stone*, *Spin*, *Billboard*, *The New York Times*, *Women's Wear Daily*, *Inked*, *Skin Deep*, *Revolver*, *HuffPost*, the *Los Angeles Times*, and hundreds more. See Figure 7–2 on page 79 for a sampling of where our brand has been featured.

FIGURE **7-2** Our Brand's Reach in Media

Of course, getting all these interviews and articles at once is impossible. We didn't do it like that, either. We got one, and then another, and then another. Most of the time, Sean would simply reach out to the publication and ask if they were interested in doing a story.

We would pitch a certain angle or an interesting take, so that it wasn't simply a "Hey, can you write an article on us?" conversation. That would have come across as arrogant or vain, neither of which is interesting to magazine or newspaper writers. Sometimes, it was "Are you interested in writing an article on our new touchscreen technology?" or "How about covering our new store location opening inside a Las Vegas casino?" We would try to find something that would be interesting to the publication's readers. Writers often need ideas for stories, and your business can be the source of those ideas, as long as they're of interest to the community.

Magazine and newspaper articles can often lead to TV coverage as well. Get enough local attention in publications, and the door can open for more. Reach out to local TV stations on a quarterly basis and ask if they need filler content for any of their programming. One idea we used several times was breaking down what getting a tattoo or piercing looks like in a safe environment. It works, and before you know it, you will have a local news crew at your business filming for a segment. It will make your company stand out in your community and add to your credibility with consumers in the area.

Club Tattoo (along with the two of us) has been featured on TV shows such as *Blue Collar Millionaires* (CNBC), *Tattoo Stories* (Fuse), *Needles & Pins* (Vice), *Ink Master* (four separate seasons on Paramount Network), *The Doctors* (ABC), *Where It's Hot* (CBS), CNN, MSNBC, MTV, and many more. TV can have an enormous impact on your business if you can manage an appearance on the right show and solidify your presence with it.

In the past 10 or 15 years, we have seen TV shows become part of pop culture like *LA Ink*, *Miami Ink*, *Black Ink Crew*, *Tattoo Nightmares*, *Ink Master*, and more. These series have showcased the tattoo and piercing industry like no other time in history, giving tattoo artists a fame that none of them would have without the aid of TV.

The biggest downside of this type of instant fame, however, is people who develop a quick "TV brand" often open their own business even though they know nothing about actually running a business. People often show up as fans, not customers.

We have turned down more TV show opportunities than we have said yes to so we could maintain our brand integrity. Getting pitched by networks and production companies usually sounds great in the beginning stages of negotiations. But being diligent in vetting any massive public exposure of your brand is imperative before you commit to a project that could undermine your brand integrity.

Production companies have asked us to create "moments" for TV shows that were much more dramatic than how we really operate at work, such as yelling at or even firing employees on camera. Some of them have wanted us to throw things at each other or get into physical altercations with our clients. If we had done these things just for the sake of getting on TV, we would have sold out not only our company but our clients as well for a mere 15 minutes of so-called fame. No thanks.

There's one final way to build your credibility for free that we talked about earlier in the book, and that's through online reviews. Reviews of your business can play a vital role in letting your community know that you exist (at the very least), and that you're better than your competitors. There are websites and apps that can add tremendous value to your business such as Google Reviews, Yelp, Instagram, Twitter, Pinterest, and, of course, Facebook. Use your business location and your social media accounts to promote your positive reviews, and invite your customers to write reviews of their own.

Potential clients will read reviews prior to visiting or spending money in your establishment. If you are not active in managing your review content and pushing for positive feedback, any negative feedback can absolutely harm your reputation. These reviews live online forever, so it requires continual maintenance and constant attention. But it is one of the least expensive forms of marketing you can do, and it may end up being one of the most productive.

BE DEPENDABLE

Be dependable and consistent in how you conduct business and build your brand. Your customers want to know what to expect when they engage with your business, so be a brand they can depend on. To do that, be consistent in how you showcase the brand marketing (with messaging and assets) and in how you treat folks (with customer service and product quality). This is why many brand names succeed for the long haul—their brands are consistent, and people know what to expect. The customer journey has been established well in advance.

It became clear to us that in order to expand Club Tattoo on a national or even regional scale, our marketing had to be clear and concise and deliver an image that expressed what Club Tattoo was in a single advertisement. This was not an easy task. We wanted to give more details and include everything we thought was important to our potential customers. Unfortunately, at the time, we thought everything we did was important, and that sometimes resulted in a confusing message.

Looking back at some of our first attempts, we can see that our advertising was a bit jumbled and chaotic. We were trying to tell too many stories at once. We needed to simplify our story and tell it clearly and quickly. By being consistent on who we were at our core, we could make sure that our clients knew what to expect before they ever walked through our doors.

FOCUS YOUR BRAND MARKETING

Focusing your marketing spend on specific brand goals lets you really put your money to work. For example, if you use your brand's marketing dollars to promote one product or particular aspect of your brand, your returns are likely to be stronger than if you sprinkled your budget across the entirety of your offerings. So, plan to narrow that focus (and that budget) on what matters most for your brand and put a tight marketing plan in place.

By the time we opened our first store in Las Vegas, we realized that our marketing lacked a consistent overall brand message. We started attending a Las Vegas trade show called "Magic" in 2000 and 2001 to purchase merchandise and apparel for our stores and began watching the branding of the apparel companies at the event.

Each of the more successful brands we studied had a consistent message and clear identity. We could tell what a brand of apparel was about and who they were trying to appeal to by their advertising images. Very quickly we knew we had to make changes in our own approach to our messaging. Figure 7–3 on page 83 shows an example of our new branding in a taxi ad.

What potential customers could expect from looking at this ad was the top tattoo and body piercers in the world to give them a great experience and a great product in a safe and clean environment where our customers' safety came first. All the ancillary items that

FIGURE 7-3 Club Tattoo Taxi Ad Featuring Thora

we offered (such as jewelry) were moved to a secondary position so we could focus on our core message. By showing a beautiful and confident woman in our ad, we are portraying a lifestyle of beauty and quality. The viewer can see that the tattoos are of high quality and that she is wearing a beautiful piece of gold in her nostril. Everything about this ad is meant to portray our studios as clean, high quality, and women friendly.

In order to implement all these key factors and make sure we would become more efficient, we started thinking and acting more like a traditional business by working with a rough budget and developing a marketing plan. Up to that point, we just did what we felt like doing when opportunities arose and made decisions based on what we "liked," or what "sounded good," not on what we knew worked. We had not yet learned how to gather or analyze empirical data to show which advertising was working and which campaigns were having little or no positive effect.

8

CUT THE EXCUSES, GET UP, AND DO SOMETHING!

s the drive to create something great a quality you are born with, or is it something you develop over time? It seems to us like the urge to create something great is an obsession at this point in our careers. Even when we are working on something simple, we think (or even say out loud), "How can we make this better?"

The ability to stop yourself and ask this question is a hallmark of a brand renegade. Sure, you may have a successful business—but how can you make it more than it is today? Elevate it to the next level? Make it stand out in the marketplace of ideas? Even if you have a good idea, you don't yet have a GREAT one. Being able to apply the brakes and re-envision your business in a unique way—or even in a way that may seem impossible—is how you build your brand. You've got to cut the excuses and just go for it.

In this chapter, we'll show you how we did just that—cut the excuses and got the damn thing done.

CHANGE CUSTOMER PERCEPTIONS, CHANGE YOUR FUTURE

As a brand renegade, you have to think outside the box of your industry. Decide what the accepted norm is, and then smash it. Follow the unexpected path, not the well-worn one. We believe it is this thought process that led us to build one of the key differentiating factors for our business model: Interactive Tattoo.

For years, the tattoo industry seemed relatively unchanged, and we always saw ourselves as just a little different. But we wanted to be better. We decided to give our customers a different experience at Club Tattoo than they would have at any other tattoo parlor in town. The idea came to us early on when we decided that we were going to change the aesthetic of the business entirely.

Most tattoo parlors in the mid-1990s were seedy little hole-in-the-wall shops in a bad part of town; they were run-down and quite intimidating to walk into. We wanted to change that. We wanted a business where everyone felt comfortable, especially women. We thought if we created an environment that women felt comfortable with, then the men would naturally follow.

So we brought in bright lighting and a clean atmosphere and called ourselves a "studio" rather than a "parlor." We wanted our business to feel more like an art gallery or upscale salon. The walls had clean, beautiful art on them, and the floors were well-maintained and looked amazing. We took the traditional "flash" (tattoo designs on paper) off the walls and put them into easily accessible books that customers could look through. We had private rooms for people who didn't want to get their tattoo or piercing in public. As simple as this sounds, it was revolutionary in the industry at the time.

WORK THROUGH THE FEAR AND JUMP INTO ACTION

What made us stand out from everyone else? Obviously, it was our actions, but beyond that, it was our ability to move forward in the face of fear. Fear is one of the most powerful (and arguably *the* most powerful) emotions. Fear drives the majority of people's decisions, especially at the small business level. It is understandable—we all worked so hard to get here, and we don't want to make a mistake that will force us to start all over again.

Fear can cause inaction, and inaction can cause your company to lose out on opportunities. The largest opportunities usually show themselves in times of crisis, when most other businesses will be paralyzed from fear. You can combine this fear with your intuition and use it to analyze the facts in front of you, come to a sound conclusion, and take decisive action. One of the greatest lessons we ever learned from Tony Robbins was that "to make massive change, it requires massive action." This could not be truer in the business universe.

Think about the financial crisis of 2007 to 2009. How many people did you know who lost their homes or businesses? It is widely known that the subprime markets were manipulated and predatory in many instances. However, it is also known that many investors walked away from these loans based on the portfolio loan-to-value ratios. Many of them probably did so through fear. Some thought that the markets would not bounce back soon enough and add back in the monetary value that they had lost on paper, so they walked away from their homes or businesses. For many people it absolutely crushed them financially and took years to recover, if at all. Many people stayed the course, hoped for a real estate rebound, and pivoted their finances into other opportunities. It was specifically in those moments of uncertainty that some entrepreneurs moved past their fear and made strategic and sound decisions for growth. Navigating financial movements through fear is not an easy thing for most people to do; many people get paralyzed and do nothing.

We made our largest company expansion during the middle of the financial meltdown when we decided to open our flagship studio on the Las Vegas Strip. We had been working several deals in Las Vegas since 2005. Initially we had been working with the Hard Rock in 2005, then we signed a lease in 2006 at the Cosmopolitan on the Las Vegas strip. After nearly two years of building delays and the financial crash that occurred in 2007 to 2008, the Cosmopolitan went into default and was taken over by Deutsche Bank. Sean had to fly up to Vegas for a meeting with the new landlord team, and it did not go well.

When Sean walked into the room for the meeting, he knew that something didn't feel right. Everyone was cold and didn't make eye contact with him. The team started to explain that under the new management team, the casino/hotel wanted to take a new direction and relocate our store that we already had our lease on. Sean explained that we were not OK with this idea and the banker team got hostile. After several minutes of uncomfortable confrontation Sean stood up in front of the team and said, "If you guys don't understand why our brand makes this property cooler, then you simply don't understand this market or us and we can go elsewhere."

We had been getting courted by several properties in Las Vegas by that time and one that stood out was the Miracle Mile Shops at Planet Hollywood, directly across the street from the Cosmopolitan. Sean simply walked across the street after his meeting with the bankers and walked the property. As Sean walked the property, he called Thora and explained the appeal and the amount of traffic he was seeing there. After a few discussions in early 2008, we took the meeting. We, along with Chester, flew into Las Vegas and for what would become a watershed moment for our company, met with the Miracle Mile landlords.

The Miracle Mile team was very energetic and understood the Club Tattoo brand appeal and were very excited to bring us into their property not simply as a tenant that pays rent but a collaborative brand that showcased the property in a newer sexier light. They understood right away that by bringing Club Tattoo into their tenant mix, that the client experience would go from a typical mall experience with brands like Build-A-Bear, to an older and more hip Vegas traveler looking for a unique experience.

We spoke with Chester and all agreed that this was the best choice for the expansion into the Las Vegas market with a new flagship studio. The studio would cost nearly $2 million to design, build, and stock and was coming with a great financial risk. While the team had approximately $1 million in cash, we had to borrow the remaining $1 million to get it completed.

Under normal circumstances, this would have been a tall order for a tattoo studio to try and accomplish, but what made it even harder is that in the middle of 2008, the banks across America, and the world, were starting to have a financial meltdown that was impacting everything and everyone. Although it was a very uncertain time for us personally and for our business, we believed in our brand and business model enough to take the risk and build in the uncertain financial environment. The fear of all of the negative possibilities could have been paralyzing had we chosen to live in it. However, we chose to capitalize on that moment of worldwide panic and trust in ourselves and what we had built together.

We opened after many hurdles on March 5, 2009, inside the Miracle Mile Shops at Planet Hollywood. The store was an immediate success, and we were so overwhelmed with business that we had to quickly scale everything up in order to meet demand. The design of the studio would not only change our business aesthetic and brand perception but created a demand for our brand in properties around the globe and gave us an international stage in which to display it to millions of visitors a year.

The biggest takeaway (although there were many lessons in this event) was for us to trust our processes and learn to move past our fear and use it as a tool for growth. Chances are, whatever you're afraid of, it probably isn't as bad as you think it is.

ALWAYS TAKE THE MEETING

Let's go back to 2007 for a moment. We were starting to get international attention with Club Tattoo through our collaborations with Etnies shoes (which we'll talk about in Chapter 12) and our business partnership with longtime friend Chester Bennington. It was time to bring our company to the next level, and we wanted to invest in our brand. We weren't sure what this meant, however, so we began bouncing ideas off one another: everything from playing music in the studios to new furniture and jewelry displays. Eventually, Sean got a phone call from a longtime acquaintance named Cristin Davis that changed our business model forever.

Cristin had known Sean for several years during their time in the Phoenix music scene. Sean played drums in Grey Daze, and Cristin played guitar in local favorite band, Big Shot Allstar, and then in another band called Trik Turner, which had some national radio success as well. Cristin had left the music scene (although he eventually joined Chester, Sean, and Mace in the reunited Grey Daze in 2016) and started a new career path in computers and software development.

One day, Cristin called Sean, saying he wanted to meet to talk about an idea he had about the tattoo industry. We get many calls and emails like this, and 99 out of 100 times, the ideas are either awful, already exist, or make no sense at all. However, we have a rule that we have lived by since the late 1990s, and it has served us well many times: Always take a meeting.

Sean met Cristin in our office at Club Tattoo in Tempe, and he explained that he wanted to take the traditional approach toward tattoo designs "flash" as it is known in the tattoo industry and throw it out the window by creating a database that was accessible via touchscreen. As we mentioned earlier, one of the first differentiating factors for Club Tattoo was that we took the "flash" off of the walls in our original concept and put the designs into organized books. This was to be the newest iteration of that original idea.

Sean liked what he was saying but had a few ideas to add to this program himself. One of the problems we had had in our business was with the presentation of our artists' portfolios. Some took enormous pride in their presentation and bought really nice photo albums to display their work in, but others didn't care how they were presented, as long as they were making money. This, of course, was a very shortsighted approach, but try arguing with a fool and see how far that gets you. With this in mind, he asked Cristin if we could also include a section where artists' and piercers' portfolios could be shown and easily updated. Cristin loved that idea and wrote it down on his notepad. He told Sean he thought he could create the program for about $20,000 to $30,000, and it would take about 120 days to complete the first prototype.

After the meeting, the two of us sat down at home and went over everything: what the program could do and what it would cost. Cristin's touchscreen concept struck us as an instant game changer. It could separate our business model from every other tattoo and piercing shop in the world and add an immense amount of value to our aesthetic model as well. Even though the program itself didn't generate revenue, it seemed like a worthwhile investment long-term because of the impact it would have on our customers' experience.

We agreed to the investment and called Cristin back to get him started on creating what would become Interactive Tattoo.

INNOVATE TO ELEVATE YOUR BRAND

After about two months, Cristin called and told us he was ready to show the progress he had made on the Interactive Tattoo program. We met at our office again, and Cristin brought a touchscreen with a computer along to show us what it did and how it worked. We went through the program and took notes on the parts we loved as well as the ones we wanted to change. Both of us could see that this was going to be an incredible tool for our company and give our clients an experience in our stores that they had never had before.

Within the 120-day deadline (or at least awfully close to it), Cristin had delivered our first two prototype Interactive Tattoo stations. We set them up in the lobby of our first location in Tempe after business hours. Cristin, with some help from his father, got the first two touchscreens installed and started testing them. We probably stayed at the store until 3 A.M. testing and playing with the new system. We could not wait to unveil it to our staff the following day.

From day one, we could see that this was, in fact, a game changer for our businesses and the Club Tattoo brand. It was apparent right away that the artists loved the system as much as the clients. Their portfolio pictures looked clean and bright and could not get stolen or destroyed. The screens could be disinfected and cleaned immediately after use unlike a physical portfolio, which might be handled hundreds of times a day by thousands of clients per month. That was a lot of unseen bacteria floating around the studio, and it was instantly gone with Interactive Tattoo. (This feature would eventually become yet another key differentiator for Club Tattoo in 2020 during the Covid-19 outbreak.)

Furthermore, multiple clients could view each artist's portfolio simultaneously. The artist could easily access a specific image by tapping on the predetermined categories we had created for them. We had started the system with approximately 7,000 images and 390 categories, such as lions, flowers, birds, etc. Of course, we knew we needed to expand the offering almost immediately. People would ask, "Do you have any pictures of this or that?" and if we didn't, we made a note to go back and add that category and art into the system the following day or week.

The system was designed so that we could update and expand it very easily. By 2020, it had expanded to more than 200,000 designs, with nearly 2,000 categories and subcategories. In addition, Cristin and Sean added a virtual text editor and instant translator that gave us multiple language options, such as German, Italian, French, Portuguese, and Spanish. It was and still is something that separates Club Tattoo from every other business in our industry.

We have always wanted to mold great ideas into great things. We put the innovative possibilities first without thinking about how it will monetize for us. Whether it is a collaboration license or a ground-up software platform that takes years to develop, we always think of how we can add value, not only to our own businesses or clients but to everyone we do business with as well. Adding value in unique and unexpected ways for our industry is one of the most important chrematistics we hold dear. We cut the excuses that are common in our industry, got off our asses, and did the damn thing—and so can you.

9

ADD "F*!%" TO YOUR BRAND VOCABULARY

elax. The word is *fail*.

We wish more people understood how many times most "overnight successes" have failed before they truly hit the big time. Overnight success is generally reserved for the lottery, not business. For every success we have had in our business, there are probably ten failures to go with it, and we are not ashamed of that in the least. We have come to understand that the failures are an essential part of our growth.

Most people fear failure. However, it is the ability to move forward in the face of that fear that makes us different. That is our definition of courage, and courage will help you focus, which will lead to decisive action. We would rather try and fail than never try at all.

Does that mean we enjoy failing? Of course not, but it does mean we try not to let it discourage us from moving forward. We use, "Try not to let it discourage" as a mantra, because we are also human, and like every human, we have our moments of doubt. But the quality that separates success from failure is the ability to keep moving forward in the face of failure—or even many failures. In this chapter, we'll tell you a bit about our experiences with the F-word (failure) and how it helped drive us to create a business brand that ultimately succeeds and stands out from its competition.

PLAN FOR FAILURE

In October 2000, the city of Tempe, Arizona, was putting forward a vote for approval of a light rail transit system. The line was to be built all the way through the city on Apache Boulevard—directly in front of our business. At the time, Sean's father was an accountant for the Arizona Department of Transportation and told us what generally happens to local businesses along the construction route. We concluded that the light rail, if it passed, would probably put us and at least 30 others out of business.

The city had an open forum to discuss the light rail funding proposal, and we attended and spoke to the mayor and members of the city council from the perspective of local business owners. Sean's father had showed us the budget numbers and pointed out the shortfalls, inconsistencies, and outright lies that the local and state government were trying to sell the citizens of Tempe. They lied about the preliminary budget, foreseen impact on local businesses, and contingency plans for mitigating unforeseen problems. Sean stood in front of the city council and pleaded our case based on these facts. But the mayor, Neil Giuliano, assured us that our numbers were "incorrect." He even called us several days later to put our minds at rest and continued to tell us that the city was going to financially assist affected businesses, so there was no need to be concerned. "The city is here to help," he told us.

Newspapers started to contact Sean for interviews immediately after the council meeting, and we began to get a lot of local attention.

Some of the dishonesty that Sean had pointed out was turning out to be true, and members of the city council were not too happy about having to answer questions.

A city council member named Ben Arredondo called us one night after Sean had done a radio interview. He was kind to us, but as we were wrapping up our conversation he advised that if Sean were a "smart boy," he would drop his public shaming of the light rail and "be quiet." Another man claiming to represent a construction company called the following week and said, "You know, son, people get hurt and even killed sometimes when messing around with government contracts. There is a lot of money at stake and a lot of things you do not understand. Be smart and shut your mouth," and then hung up.

In the end, all our efforts didn't matter. In 2005, they began three years of construction on less than 2.5 miles of road. The initial budget was $587 million, and the final cost ended up around $1.4 billion. Forty-one businesses on Apache Boulevard and Terrace Road went under during those three years; none of them ever received any government assistance that we are aware of.

Our business survived solely on the basis of the brand we had built, our perseverance in making sure our clients knew about the construction hazards ahead of time, and the fact that we saw it coming years in advance and **planned for failure.**

We had realized that when the light rail construction started, it would impact our business so much that we would almost certainly have to close, so we immediately started looking for a new location. After several months, we found an old music store three blocks away that had just been bought out of foreclosure by an investment firm. We negotiated a lease and began construction within five months of losing the battle on the light rail.

YOU CAN'T RE-CREATE THE WHEEL—BUT YOU CAN BUILD A NEW ONE

We took our first large business loan by securing a business line of credit for $120,000 and used $80,000 of our own cash. We were taking an enormous gamble on opening another studio so close to our first store, but deep down we knew it was the right choice. We used almost all the money to build out the new studio, furniture, equipment, jewelry, and displays. We repainted the outside of the building and stained the concrete inside. It was truly a beautiful store when we were finished.

Our friend and Sean's mentor, Kerry Rose, had told us that going from your first location to your second will be the hardest thing you do in business. We didn't quite understand what he meant at the time. We assumed we would just do what we did to create the first store, and everything would work out fine.

What we didn't understand is that it took years to build our first studio into what it had become, and to duplicate that process in a few short months would be extremely demanding. The second store had to be as good as or even better than the first store as soon as it opened. Both of us kept Kerry's advice in mind as we had long conversations about our goals and what steps we were going to take to make those goals a reality.

If there is any one piece of advice we can give future brand renegades about opening a second location or scaling your brand, it is this: Write down every single necessary process, piece of equipment, tool, furniture, and protocol *before you start*. It is incredibly difficult to try to re-create your business without first understanding how you built it in the first place. What seems like second nature will quickly become a tangled mystery if you don't clearly define your process for everything—in writing.

DON'T LET FEAR DRIVE YOUR EMOTIONS

Our biggest hurdle during the process was lacking trust in each other to complete our assigned responsibilities. At one point our tension built up so high that when I (Thora) challenged something Sean was doing with the jewelry display cases, he threw a roll of paper towels at me out of sheer frustration. This sent me into a rage and I was about to attack him when suddenly the front door flew open, and Keith, one of the new tattoo artists, arrived to help put the shop together.

Keith coming in may have saved us from having an actual physical fight that neither of us really wanted. We were just stressed beyond the point of understanding and our coping skills were depleted.

That was the moment that we realized we couldn't keep going without setting some new ground rules. I felt Sean was overbearing in his expectations of me, but I also knew I had a tendency to be controlling.

We both had to learn how to "let go" and trust each other with our roles and capabilities. By no means did this happen overnight; we still struggle with it at times. But we both acknowledge that each of us has a defined role in the company, and we have to respect each other's ability to get things done. By micromanaging each other, we caused unnecessary conflict and lost the trust of our partner.

When we finally did open the second studio, it took several months for business to pick up, and we couldn't understand why. In our rush to forestall the light rail crisis that was still unfolding, we had not realized that having a studio so close to the original location would be a difficult sell to our current clients. Although we felt that we were eventually going to close the first studio location due to the light rail, we thought having another location would still be beneficial, regardless of the proximity to the first due to our overflow traffic at that time. We had opened this second studio literally three blocks away from our original location. Our fans and clients knew and were comfortable with the reputation of our first studio and the artists and piercers who worked there. Our newest studio was not immediately accepted by our clientele, even though it was so close, because it was still unknown.

We had to create a new client base, and we had to do it in the same physical radius as our first studio. It took about a year of consistent advertising and brand messaging to get the second location to take off, but once it did, our company would never be the same. By planning for the failure of our first location (or, rather, planning for the destructive impact of the light rail construction), we safeguarded the future success of Club Tattoo. In the end, our second location held the foundation for our company and allowed us to remain open throughout the construction period of the light rail. We were one of the few businesses that didn't have to close because of the light rail and came through it relatively unscathed. We wish we could say the same for the other businesses on the light rail path. Every business in our immediate plaza had either shut down or been sold due to the construction invasiveness. We would eventually sell our first location in 2011 to a competitor as we expanded into other locations.

FOCUS ON THE RESULT YOU WANT—NOT YOUR FEAR OF FAILURE

One of the boldest moves in our business growth process, and one that many insisted was too large for us to take on, was our first purchase of commercial property. Almost a year after we moved into our second location, our new landlord, Joe, approached us and explained that his investment firm wanted to free up some cash by liquidating our building. We started to get a little nervous as we realized that a new landlord might not want a tattoo studio as a tenant, and we could lose the location and the large investment we had just made altogether.

We started doing the math to see whether we could afford to buy the building. Joe agreed to sell it to us at its appraised value, which came in at $390,000. But when Sean called him to let him know the results of the appraisal, Joe started having second thoughts about selling the building so "inexpensively."

Joe had purchased the building through bank repossession one year earlier for $180,000, and we had put $100,000 into the tenant build out, improving the value of the property. He was going to double his money in less than a year. Sean was furious and wouldn't speak to Joe for a couple of weeks.

In the end, Sean agreed to sit down and negotiate with Joe, who told us candidly that sometimes one party holds all the leverage, and the other party must bow to that leverage or miss out on the deal. We were not used to being on the downside of a business deal, and it was an extremely hard pill for us to swallow. Sean wanted to reach across the table and knock his teeth out, but he knew that wouldn't get us what we wanted, which was the building.

Before the meeting, we recalled a principle from one of our favorite books, *The 7 Habits of Highly Effective People* by Stephen Covey: Begin with the end in mind. In other words, when you know what you want the end result to be, concentrate on that and nothing else. The three of us negotiated a price of $450,000 for the building, and everyone left the table happy. We saved up approximately $90,000 in cash over the next four months for our down payment, Joe carried the extra $60,000 over the appraised value, and we paid off the loan within three years.

As of 2021, the building had a market value of $5 million, and we have received several offers even higher. It was one of the best investments of our career. The lesson was clear for us: Keep your emotions out of the business deal and focus on the result you want. Nothing else matters.

SOMETIMES DOING THE RIGHT THING CAN STILL MEAN FAILURE

About the same time (around 2006), the state of Arizona wanted to implement new health and safety laws pertaining to the tattoo and piercing industry. A Democratic state senator named Meg Burton Cahill and a Democratic state representative named David Schapira reached out to Sean by phone and asked if he would come to the State Capitol building for a brief meeting. Sean agreed, and a week or so later he made the trip and was ushered into a large conference room where he met both the senator and the representative along with their teams. Senator Cahill briefly explained that they wanted Sean to help them write and define the new health laws for the industry.

Although the meeting went well, we felt there should be many more industry experts involved in writing the law, so the following week, Sean rented out a hotel conference room and invited about 50 of the leading tattoo and piercing studio owners we knew to come share their ideas.

Our intention was to create something sensible and to make sure everyone had a voice in the matter. We certainly did not want to make enemies in our industry. Keep in mind that in 2006, there were absolutely no health regulations for the tattoo or piercing industry in Arizona other than age requirements.

The other shop owners met with us several times over the coming months, and within a year, we had created a 54-page bill with Senator Cahill and Representative Schapira that would increase the baseline standards for the industry by maintaining sterilization records, installing a clean hand-washing station in each business, and requiring updated record keeping, inspections, and minimum training for each licensee. All the changes were self-funded by our industry. It made practical sense, and all the tattoo shop owners who had been involved agreed on the rules we had created. It was smart, safe, and, most important, it secured the future of the tattoo and piercing industry in a meaningful way.

As we wound up the work on the new Tattoo and Piercing Health Bill, Representative Schapira asked Sean to introduce the bill to the committee at the Arizona House of Representatives. Sean was flattered and nervous, to say the least, but we had put more than a year's worth of work into it and wanted to see it through. He agreed to present the bill to the house and dressed to impress that morning. He brought our friend Sage, who owned another tattoo studio, with him to the meeting, and together they entered the committee forum with proud smiles on their faces.

As Sean was waiting for his moment, Rep. Schapira motioned for him to come over, leaned in, and whispered, "We didn't think that we could get the committee to approve the bill for a vote the way you guys wrote it, so my team took the liberty of rewriting it last night. Here it is." He then handed Sean a bill that removed all the common-sense measures and safety mechanisms and left only the part where our industry members would have to pay for licensing on a yearly basis.

Sean sat there in shock. He didn't know what to do. He was about to get up and speak before the committee—and it was televised as well. Rep. Schapira sat right next to him and smiled as if nothing was wrong. As he stood up and approached the podium to introduce Sean, Sean's heart sank. He told the committee who Sean was, his expertise within the industry, and the bill he was going to introduce.

Sean's heart pounded as he stood up and thanked Schapira for the introduction and went on to describe his years in business in the Tempe community. He told them how long our team had worked on the bill and what their intentions were, as the committee listened intently. All the attributes of what we had worked on and completed were explained in detail to the committee as they watched and listed to him intently. That was the moment Sean decided to do what no one in the room thought that he would. He decided to do the right thing.

Sean told the committee that Cahill and Schapira had double-crossed not just him, but more importantly the entire industry, which had written and supported the bill these two had rewritten at the last minute. He asked them to vote "No" on the bill and let the entire committee know how upset we were that we had all wasted a year of our time and energy. He also let them know how disappointed we were, because we genuinely wanted to improve our industry, and the committee had thrown it out the window.

The chairman was confused and asked Sean, "Sir, are you here presenting this bill that YOU worked on only to ask us to deny it for presentation to the House of Representatives?"

Sean answered, "Yes, sir, I am. I am asking you to vote this bill down today," and walked off the floor. Rep. Schapira was furious and left the room just flicking his hand in the air as if to brush us off—and as if we had let HIM down! The vote from the committee was a unanimous "No," and the bill was defeated.

We know we stood up for our industry that day, and we did what was right. The easier thing would have been to stand in front of that committee and say the usual words, and the bill would have passed, but what they did was wrong, and we wanted nothing to do with it. Sean later received a phone call from Senator Cahill wanting him to explain why he changed his mind on the bill. Sean didn't bother calling her back. She was there. She knew what had happened.

BEWARE OF ULTERIOR MOTIVES

Approximately three months after we put the health bill to rest, we were busy building our company when we received a very strange visit from a very well-known man. In the summer of of the mid-2000s, a United States senator came into Club Tattoo in Tempe and asked if he could have a few minutes of Sean's time. Sean had recognized him the moment he walked in. The senator was a well-known figure in Arizona for many years.

The senator explained to Sean that he had been working as a lobbyist (and sits on the board of directors) for several companies in the country and had been reading about our health and safety bill. He told Sean he thought he could help get the actual bill we had written voted into law. He wanted to see the "folks" in Arizona be able to raise the standards of our business community. He spoke of how impressed he was that Sean was so young and so driven to improve our industry. He was a true politician inside and out.

Sean was still trying to figure out why we had a U.S. senator sitting in our office at our tattoo studio. We were confused. That is, until he explained that if we were to pay his consulting business $7,000 per month for eight to ten months, he would make calls to his friends and associates at the state level, get the bill reintroduced in committee, and eventually passed in the state legislature. He also let us know that we could add clauses into it that specifically benefited us if we wanted to.

Sean was in shock. This man had just asked for a bribe, and he wasn't dancing around the issue. We realized that he just viewed us as lowlifes in a seedy industry and did not have respect for us at all. He just wanted to soak us for as much money as he could.

But there was no way we were going to bribe a U.S. senator for a state-level health and safety bill that should have been passed on its own merit. Sean called the senator's consulting firm and left a message for him, politely declining his offer to work with our company. To no one's surprise, he never called us back.

10

BE POWERFUL LEADERS, NOT BOSSES

One of the most common misconceptions that small-business owners express to us (usually while conversing with us about starting their own business) is the concept that owning their own business is going to be less work than working for someone else. Nothing could be further from the truth. As a matter of fact, when this is said (and believe us, it is said quite often), we try as hard as we can to talk them out of opening their own business. We tell them in a very straightforward way, "Don't do it. You may not have what it takes to become a business owner with that mindset." Sometimes that statement can be hurtful. We certainly do not want to ever discourage someone's dreams; however, we must give honest feedback and advice.

Many people are disillusioned with the freedom they see from other entrepreneurs but fail to see the many hours of hard work that they put in to achieve that level of freedom. Furthermore, every successful entrepreneur that we have ever had the pleasure of doing business or speaking with never dreamed about the freedom that comes with being successful. They dreamt instead of creating something special, something different, and something great.

At least in our case, we know in our hearts that we can say that unequivocally. We never chased a dream of freedom, vacations, or money. Our only mission when starting the company was to pursue greatness. We never even thought about making money or becoming rich. In fact, the only thoughts we had about money related to paying bills, buying equipment, inventory, and expanding the company. It wasn't until we had been in business for well over 15 years and had an established record of grooming the businesses for success that we even approached and gave any sort of attention to the subject of money. Once we realized we actually had money, we understood it was an entirely new responsibility that had to be respected.

This principle is crucial to understand when opening your own business. If your mind is wandering about the stuff you are going to buy or the vacations you want to take once you make it rich, then you have already lost the key ingredient for success: passion. Very few entrepreneurs ever make it to the super successful stage of business ownership, and those who have are the hardest working individuals you will ever come across. They are often accused of being obsessed, one-track minded, and in love with their own businesses. In most cases, those accusations are true, and unfortunately, they are necessary for those individuals to become as successful as they have. Those humans have developed and realized their passion.

Without the passion that drives most entrepreneurs, they couldn't have gotten through the rough times that every entrepreneur will eventually and must encounter. Most of us have hit low spots or been overcome with failures that at the time didn't seem like they could be overcome. It is the passion and desire of the true entrepreneur that has gotten those people through the rough times. It is those rough times and failures that are the driving forces that cause successful entrepreneurs to rise above and, over time, become great success stories. In this chapter, we're going to address how all these factors (work ethic, passion, and drive) help you elevate your brand by focusing on being a great leader.

WANNA BE A LEADER? PUT IN THE WORK

When we started Club Tattoo in 1995, we were naïve, as most business owners are, but had a work ethic that pushed us through. It took us a couple years and a ton of failures to realize that without the work ethic, passion, and drive, the business would have failed long ago. We realized over time that becoming a good leader had more to do with proving how hard we were willing to work than it did with trying to "motivate others." Powerful words can get lost or forgotten over time, but our staff was more inclined to learn and respond to our leadership from watching how hard we were willing to work ourselves. It was far more internal than external for us.

These qualities that were sewn into the fabric of our business model were our saving grace, and it got us through tough times and without a doubt, kept us from throwing in the towel when failure loomed over the company. Because we believed failure wasn't an option and we knew that if we quit, we would lose everything, we were ultimately faced with the truth that working harder was the only thing that was going to make our business work and succeed. Our employees (for the most part) could see this too and, in turn, were willing to put in extra work and effort as well.

HARNESS THE POWER OF YOUR PASSION

There are people who have become successful simply by working the numbers: If they sell X for 20 percent more than they pay for it, they can make money. This book is not about them; to be honest, we don't know any of those types of people. Make sure that before you start a business, you have a passion and even an obsession for whatever it is you are thinking about starting. After you have established that, work out your business plan, not the other way around.

Do not go into business half-heartedly and think you are going to succeed. It will be too easy to quit, make excuses, and watch it fail as you justify why it's someone else's fault. Your new business will take every ounce of energy that you have and more. When you come to this realization and understand the true concept of entrepreneurialism and what makes it work, it will come as no surprise that we are the only ones crazy enough to work 80 hours a week for ourselves so that we don't have to work 40 hours a week for someone else! It is the opportunity for complete freedom that drives us to work harder and, in many cases, for less money than we could make working for some other company. But the freedom is intoxicating, and the opportunities can become addictive. The chance to create something unique and do something well drives our passion and pushes us forward.

LEAN INTO YOUR CURIOSITY

We absolutely love learning something new, especially from someone who doesn't realize they are teaching us. Many times, we learn the most from our employees. There is no quality more important to a good leader than the willingness to learn and try new things, not only in their company but in their lives as well. According to the late John F. Kennedy, leadership and learning are essential to one another.

The other side of learning as much as we can is making sure that we teach as many people as possible the skills we have acquired. There is no better feeling than watching someone you employed for many years move on to something better, knowing that you helped them achieve their goals. Pride can be a beautiful thing.

FIND AND GIVE INSPIRATION

Inspiring those around us has been a life goal of ours for many years now. For a long time, we didn't fully understand the impact we had on those around us. We would sometimes feel like we were bragging while talking about our business or our lives, so we would try to downplay our story, but more often than not friends and even strangers would tell us both how inspired they were by watching our work in the community, hearing our story on TV, or reading an article about us. It was honestly remarkable that we were touching so many people and inspiring others to make a difference in their life.

Sean knows how important it was for his grandfather to give him hope for success when he was growing up, so he wants to make sure that he gives a part of himself back to the community and our employees. When we have staff meetings, we like to start with things that need work and areas that need improvement, so the staff can digest the information and get a feel for where we are coming from.

Then we change the direction of the agenda entirely and inject energy into the room by calling out individuals and recognizing moments of greatness among our staff. Whether it was an exceptional customer experience one of our clients shared about a staff member, making a great sale, or completing a beautiful tattoo, we make sure to recognize the person responsible for it. We celebrate the successes of others and make sure their peers get to not only observe it but also take part in celebrating that person.

This generally gives the staff a boost of confidence and allows them to buy into our program that much more. We make sure our team feels ownership of their accomplishments in the company. It is important to know that success is based on their hard work and enthusiasm. Whether everyone owns a piece of equity, you operate on a bonus system, or you use a commission-based system, generating enthusiasm for the hard work you are all putting in is essential. Inspiring your staff is important for focusing on short-term goals as well as long-term ones.

We always end our company meetings by encouraging feedback from the staff, no matter how silly or unimportant they might think their input may be. Sometimes what one person feels is a foolish question or suggestion can turn out to be a uniquely brilliant perspective that hadn't been considered before. We implemented a system to incentivize our staff, based on a great recommendation by a sales team member. If a staff member received more than ten positive reviews in one month, they received a financial bonus. This of course made our staff very motivated to push our clients for honest and positive reviews and increased our SEO and online presence rather quickly. Most of the team jumped at the chance to earn a bonus each month, and for a relatively small monetary investment on our part, the company culture and teamwork was positively impacted and remains to be a huge part of our business to this day.

COMMUNICATE WITH YOUR TEAM EARLY AND OFTEN

In the early years of the business, we undervalued the importance of communicating with our staff. We hadn't realized that our employees couldn't automatically know what was expected of them. Imagine that. We may feel like our goals are obvious to our teams, but we have found that if we are met with blank stares, we need to start over and explain it differently without getting frustrated. To do this we needed self-control, empathy, and lots of practice. This took time, and to be honest, it is still a work in progress.

If you have had this experience with your staff, you may want to work on developing your communication skills. Describe your goals, directions, and expectations clearly and succinctly. Be able to explain your vision to your team. You should also work on being approachable by meeting regularly with your team, interacting with them on a personal level, and having an open-door policy. Once our staff learned to trust and depend on us, they became willing to work harder for the company.

The largest contributor to our employees' enthusiasm is that they can see us doing whatever needs to be done. We are willing to pick up our parking lot, sweep the lobby floor, or organize the jewelry cases. We still have a passion for doing every job in our company (OK, maybe our passion for cleaning the bathrooms has waned just a bit). We never ask our staff to do anything that we wouldn't do.

We try to make sure our staff understands that we are always looking for ways to improve our business, our customers' experience, and our employees' happiness. Make sure they know they are doing a great job—and, just as important, make sure they understand that YOU know they are doing a great job.

Listening to your staff is vital to the success of any company. Your employees will respond to a good leader if they feel their input matters. People feel the need to be validated far more than the need to be paid well. They will leave due to bad leadership over financial gain eight out of ten times. If you can accomplish both good leadership and fair compensation, you will create a lifetime employee and team member who takes ownership of their role in your business.

DELEGATE TO EMPOWER YOUR TEAM

In addition to listening to and celebrating your staff, it is equally important to promote your staff. Our "All Star" employees crave more responsibilities and want to grow constantly. Make sure that you know which employees want more responsibility (not just the title of authority) so you can "feed" their growth and career.

The importance of learning how to delegate is often overlooked or undervalued by business owners. Many don't know how to let go of the control mechanisms that helped them succeed in the first place. Realizing your brand vision is important, but learning how to delegate the actions needed to grow and maintain that vision is crucial for creating a structured, well-organized business. If you don't learn to depend on your team, you may never progress to the next stage of business success. Trusting your team with your vision is a sign of strength, not weakness. You get credit for the people you surround yourself with.

The ability to delegate tasks to the correct person or department is one of the most important skills you can develop as your business grows. As projects and responsibilities begin to pile up, you will stretch yourself thin and become less productive, and the quality of your work will suffer. It is a rule of business: learn to let go of the small things so you can concentrate on the bigger picture.

Know When to Delegate to Your Partner

We have always worked amazingly well together when we were both rowing our boat in the same direction. However, there have been many times when we wanted two different results, or wanted the same result but disagreed on how to achieve it. Nothing can be more frustrating than having a partner who you trust but disagree with. Not knowing how to deal with that situation caused us many problems over the years. We had to learn how to delegate to each other.

Sean finally learned that he had to trust my process and let me thrive in the areas where my strengths lay, while I had to learn to let Sean be the visionary he was. Sean would usually come up with the broad ideas and direction he wanted the company to grow, and then I would help figure out the details of how to get there with the resources we had available at the time.

Although there have been many times we've adamantly disagreed, in the end we make fantastic business partners who can deal with each other honestly and respectfully. The goal for us now is finding ways to contribute to our family, friends, and community.

GIVE BACK IN AN IMPACTFUL WAY

We no longer worry about buying possessions or making large purchases other than a home; we are very content with our "stuff." Although our company has made tens of millions of dollars, the things that are most valuable to us now are the moments that we get to share with our family and giving back to our world in an impactful way.

We have always given to charity, but it was mostly around the holidays, and it was always what we thought we could afford to give at the moment. The way we approach giving now is quite different. Now we make sure that we give as much as we can as often as we can. (We'll talk more about this in Chapter 17.)

We want to leave a lasting impression on those people in our lives that we have had the absolute privilege of working with:

our employees and business partners. These people have made a meaningful impact on our lives, and we have developed some of the greatest friendships we could have ever hoped for. It is equally important for us to give back while we are still on this earth. For every great moment in our lives, we would like to create one for someone else. For us, this is one of the key components to becoming a great leader.

11

LEAVE IT BETTER THAN YOU FOUND IT

B oth of us grew up in the early 1970s and 1980s in lower-middle-class families. Both of our parents worked a 9-to-5 job at their respective employers and gave 100 percent to their daily tasks. Both put in great effort to make sure they kept their jobs and provided for their families.

Our parents taught us to work hard and make sure we understood the importance of putting 100 percent effort into everything we tried. But it was Sean's grandfather, Russell, who taught him to dream, and who helped him understand that to achieve those big dreams, he needed to find others who would be able to help get him there. He found that the best way to do that was simply by offering his services to others; eventually they would recognize the value of what he brought to the table and help him get what he needed.

In this chapter, we'll cover the concept of creating lasting value and why it's a vital building block for any smart brand renegade who wants to leave everything better than they found it.

HOW TO CREATE VALUE WITHIN YOUR BRAND

We want to emphasize that we did not chase after money to become successful. What we were really chasing was *value*. We wanted to create a company or product that had value to us and our customers, whether that was in the quality of a client's tattoo or piercing, simple confidence in our company's mission statement, or a belief that we would treat the client well. Ultimately, it was our quest for value that drove us to perfect our brand and our place in the industry.

We won't lie and say that money wasn't important, but we can say that value mattered more. If we could create a belief of our value in consumers' minds, then the money would follow. We knew that if someone getting a tattoo or piercing from Club Tattoo had an impression of our brand that held value beyond the actual tattoo or piercing itself, then we could create lifelong brand supporters instead of just counting clients. We were creating a differentiating experience for each client that gave them a confidence in our brand's quality that carries through to this day.

There were always moments where we doubted whether we were taking the brand in the right direction, but we firmly believed that simply being better and holding ourselves to a higher standard would be enough to make the difference. The following are some ways we added value to our brand.

Invest in the Customer Experience

We wanted to create the ultimate client experience, from the moment the client walked into our studio and saw how beautiful and comfortable it was, all the way to the point when we got to see the client's face looking in the mirror at their finished tattoo or piercing for the first time. We learned that those moments are where our true value was created in the customer experience.

We often spent money on equipment that we might not have needed simply because we wanted to have the best available to our staff and make sure that their impression was that we cared about our business so much that we were willing to make improvements, even when they weren't absolutely necessary. We remodeled our stores several times when they still looked fine. We simply wanted the brand to look and feel that much better and to separate us from our competition.

The other tattoo studios in the Arizona markets never put the same time, money, and energy into the way their stores looked because they didn't see the value in it. They were (and most still are) noticeably shortsighted and only cared about their bottom line.

Invest in First Impressions

There was value in making our studios look like the high-end retail stores such as Louis Vuitton, Neiman Marcus, and Dolce & Gabbana. As soon as prospective customers walked into one of our studios, they gained a sense of confidence in our brand that had never been seen before in our industry. Clients felt reassured by the high-quality look and feel of the establishments, as well as the upscale offerings of jewelry, tattoos, and piercings. Figure 11–1 on page 118 shows the high-end aesthetic of one of our Club Tattoo studios.

No one in our industry before us had designed tattoo and piercing studios to look like high-end jewelry stores or art galleries. It was truly a game changer.

> SEAN: *This was one of the biggest items of value that Thora brought to our company. Her attention to detail and design was on another level entirely and brought Club Tattoo to the very top of our industry.*

Invest in Hiring the Right People

Another area of adding value in our company was through our artists' and body piercers' experience. When we hired for an artist or piercer position, we would bring the potential contractor into our

FIGURE **11-1** A Warm Welcome at Club Tattoo

studio for an interview and show them around so they could see how the studio worked. We explained what we did for the artists and piercers in terms of marketing them and getting them aligned with us in our brand messaging.

We always felt that it was almost as important to do this exercise with those we *didn't* hire as with those we did. Even if we didn't hire them, they would get to see what an amazing business we were running, and they would eventually be busting their ass to get hired at our studio. Many times, in an interview an artist has begun telling us how much they have admired our business or how they have always dreamed about working for our company. They would often describe it as their dream job, and it was always important to us to try to live up to that for our staff. The end goal was to hire not only the artist and body piercer with the most talent but someone who could understand and adapt to our company culture. This may seem like an easy thing to ask for in today's workplace, but in the tattoo and piercing industry, it was a relatively unknown concept. The idea of curated customer experiences was something that had to be taught, and we needed candidates that could be taught and wanted to learn more in order to become better and have a better career experience.

Invest in Staff Appreciation

We believe most of our staff, if not all of them, see that we appreciate them through how we deal with our employees, facilities, and marketing. Our third year in business, we invited our staff over to our house for a Christmas celebration. We crammed everyone into the back yard of our tiny condo in Tempe and served them all dinner.

From that very first party to this day, we throw an intimate holiday party for the staff in Arizona and another party in Las Vegas. Of course, the party has been upgraded a great deal over the years. It's another way for the two of us to show them how much we appreciate their efforts throughout the year and give them a chance to get to know us outside work. We understand that by adding value in our staff's eyes, they will hopefully appreciate their jobs, work that much harder, and become more loyal and productive employees.

ADD VALUE WITH STRATEGIC PARTNERSHIPS

Once you create strong value within your brand, you can add value with outside stakeholders. Over our entrepreneurial careers, we have had the opportunity to collaborate with other well-known brands such as Harley-Davidson, Etnies, Red Monkey, Monster Energy Drink, Miracle Mile Shops LV, The Cosmopolitan, The Grand Canal Shoppes at the Venetian, Oster, Boldface Gear, Caesars Entertainment, and more. When these companies would approach us, the pitch we overwhelmingly received was that Club Tattoo would bring a sense of "cool" or "edginess" to their brands. All these companies were much larger and much more successful on the global scale than Club Tattoo, but they understood that our brand would add an inherent value to theirs.

In 2011, for example, we were approached by Bicycle, the world's leading maker of playing cards. They set up a conference call between us and their creative team and explained that they had found us on the internet and were impressed with our market presence.

They wanted to buy our tattoo designs for an upcoming card deck. While listening to their pitch, we began thinking about how to add value to their idea. Selling our tattoo designs to them was simple enough, and we could have made a little money on the project, but we wanted it to be awesome, and we wanted our name on it.

As the ideas flowed, Sean politely interrupted and asked, "How would anyone buying these decks know that they are legitimate tattoo designs? Any collector would not just trust some company that put out a tattoo-style deck of cards. Why don't you do a collaboration with Club Tattoo, and make it a Club Tattoo deck of cards by Bicycle instead of just buying our artwork?" They loved the idea, and the entire direction of the project refocused on making it happen. We collaborated on the designs with a couple of artists at our Las Vegas location, and within four months we had the designs ready for the deck, which you can see in Figure 11–2 on page 121.

The decks were an instant hit, and they were picked up by Bicycle's largest retailers, including Walmart, Target, Walgreens, and many more. The decks ended up selling more than 230,000 units worldwide and were such a success that Bicycle had us do a second deck, which launched in 2016. These deals never would have happened if the company hadn't shared its vision with us and been able to see the value we brought to the table.

From the Bicycle collaboration, we were approached by another company called Oster. Oster was owned by its parent company (at the time) Jarden, which also owns Bicycle and many other companies. We went through a similar process of getting to know the Oster design team and trying to understand what they were looking for and how we could help them achieve that.

Within a few conversations, we knew we could best add value by designing tattoo art for their hair clipper line. There was a strong subcultural movement in the barber and hair professionals industry that closely aligned with a tattooed lifestyle. Heavily tattooed and pierced hair professionals were trending at an incredibly fast rate,

FIGURE 11-2 First- and Second-Generation Club Tattoo Playing Cards

and the hair product industry wanted to capitalize on it as quickly as possible. We wanted to create a product that spoke to these individuals about their creativity while putting a spotlight on their tattoos and artistic flair.

FIGURE **11-3** Club Tattoo Oster Clippers

Oster and Club Tattoo launched a collaboration series of hair clippers (shown in Figure 11–3 above) in 2016 at the world's largest hair show in Las Vegas. They sold more than 40,000 units and generated more than $1 million in revenue.

Our success in the strategic partnership arena continued, and in 2017, Club Tattoo and Boldface Gear (an accessories company) came together to launch a new style of backpack for the Boldface brand. Boldface wanted to create something that mid-to-late teens could relate to artistically while keeping a certain sense of street credibility. Their president, Randy Fenton, realized after a brief phone call with us that Club Tattoo could bring an entirely new value to a collaboration. The backpacks launched in November 2017, and we got getting tremendous feedback from day one. You can see some examples of them in Figure 11–4 on page 123.

The main reason we love opportunities like these so much is that we get a chance to show these global companies how we can align our brand with theirs and add value to what they are doing. We never worried about making money on these deals on the front end— we just focused on making sure that our brand alignment added value to both companies. The global exposure we have received by participating in these collaborations is far more valuable than the

FIGURE **11-4** Boldface Gear's Club Tattoo Collection

money we made from them. They made Club Tattoo part of the global conversation and helped separate us from the rest of the tattoo and piercing industry.

PUT YOUR VALUES AND MISSION IN WRITING

While creating a mission statement is standard practice for most businesses when they are starting out, we think it's important for brand renegades to re-envision the importance of such a statement. If you want to elevate your brand above the industry fray, you have to create a mission statement that goes beyond the basics of "here's who we are and what we do." Instead, it needs to speak to the brand identity you are creating so you can use it as a value touchpoint for your customers, staff, and strategic partners.

The sidebar on page 125 contains the mission statement we wrote for Club Tattoo. It describes how we perceive our company bringing value to the marketplace. If you have not already created a mission statement for your company, do so now, focusing on the value of your brand identity. If you already have one, take a look at it with new eyes and see if you can improve or update it from this point of view. When you are focused on trying to add value to the people around you, it creates a much more fulfilling life—and a stronger company.

CLUB TATTOO'S MISSION STATEMENT

Club Tattoo has redefined the luxury tattoo and piercing industry by creating a viable lifestyle that reaches a wide audience but maintains a core value system that is innovative and has set a new standard for the tattoo and piercing industry.

We have pioneered a level of sterility, cleanliness, and professionalism that is unique in the tattoo and body piercing industry that appeals to a wider variety of consumers.

We pride ourselves on being the utmost discerning when choosing tattoo artists and professional body piercers to represent our brand and maintain the integrity of quality and professionalism needed to meet the demand of a mainstream audience.

Our primary goal is to ensure that our customers have a safe, enjoyable, comfortable, and, hopefully, life-changing experience while getting a permanent piece of body art, body piercing, or simply dabbling in our lifestyle by purchasing unique fashion or jewelry that we offer as part of the Club Tattoo experience.

There is something for everyone at Club Tattoo!

A visit to Club Tattoo will create a lasting impression on the idea of body art and set a new standard for what you should expect when seeking it.

12

IT IS NOT ABOUT THE MONEY

Throughout our 25-plus years in business, we have had many opportunities to partner with other individuals, companies, and regional governments. One factor that has contributed to our many successful partnerships is that we generally don't take on a business venture unless we are passionate about the concept or feel that we can enhance or add value to it. In this chapter, we'll talk about what drives us to invest in outside ventures as brand renegades.

GOING INTERNATIONAL

We came across our first opportunity for an international business collaboration in 2004. We had just partnered with longtime friend and Linkin Park singer Chester Bennington and had expanded to three locations in the Phoenix metropolitan area. We had begun to develop a real brand with Club Tattoo that people could engage and identify with. Business opportunities were starting to present themselves rather quickly.

In early 2004, a representative from Sole Technology, the world's fourth-largest shoe company, contacted Chester about doing a signature line of shoes. He didn't want to just put his name on a shoe, as many athletes and rock stars did at the time, so he reached out to us about doing the collaboration with Club Tattoo instead to provide artwork for Sole Technology's Etnies shoe line. The idea sounded intriguing, so we went back and forth with the Etnies team to try to understand their vision and eventually came to an understanding that we would create custom tattoo artwork for their men's and women's shoe line. There was nothing like this on the market at the time. It felt like a once-in-a-lifetime opportunity, and we did not want to mess it up, especially because Chester had passed on a chance to create his own signature line and brought it to us instead. If we did well in our presentation, we knew that other doors would begin opening quickly.

Over the next 45 days, we worked with our group of artists on the designs for the new shoe line. We quickly discovered that a design that looks great on paper doesn't necessarily look good once you wrap it onto the contour of a shoe. This would prove to be one of our biggest challenges in the design process.

Our team eventually created about 40 design concepts that worked well, and we felt like we were ready to present to the Etnies team. In May, we booked a flight and met with Chester and the entire creative team at Sole Technology, who were very warm, inviting, and excited about the project.

When we sat down for the meeting, we had actually mocked up our designs on their shoe model templates with different color variations, sizes, and placement options. You can see one of these designs in Figure 12–1 on page 129. Their team was blown away by how prepared we were for the meeting and kept commenting that they

FIGURE **12-1** One of Our Etnies Shoe Designs

never got to work with partners who showed up so well-prepared. The three of us were surprised—for us, this level of preparedness was simple common sense. Just showing up with art on paper would have been underwhelming and disconnected to the overall project.

It is important when entering any collaboration to demonstrate that you understand your business partner. It will give you a better starting point and create value more easily for you and your team. Do your homework and find out where your skill set can add value in the project.

By the end of the meeting, the Etnies team decided they wanted to go from one men's and one women's shoe to a three-year deal where Etnies would cobrand their shoes with Club Tattoo and create a total of four men's and four women's shoes. The first set of the Club Tattoo/Etnies shoe collaboration debuted at the ASR trade show in San Diego in fall 2004. The shoe collection would go on to become one of the most successful collaborations Etnies ever did, and we are immensely proud of it to this day. You can still find them on social media as a collectible. You can see some more of our shoe designs in Figure 12–2 below.

FIGURE **12-2** More Club Tattoo Etnies Shoe Designs

LET INNOVATION LEAD YOU

The largest apparel show in the world is called "Magic," and it is held twice a year in fabulous Las Vegas. Sean was at Magic in 2005 (where we would look at the newest on-trend fashion to purchase for our studios) when fellow entrepreneur Vanessa Nornberg approached him about designing a new piece of jewelry for her manufacturing company, Metal Mafia.

Sean teaches different body piercing techniques around the world and had become one of the industry's leaders. He was widely respected among the absolute best in the field, and he had recently developed a piercing technique for a brand-new type of body piercing called a microdermal anchor.

A *microdermal anchor* is a body piercing that sits directly under the skin and has only one point of exit from the body. Traditional piercings have two exit points so that the jewelry enters and exits the body. This new type of piercing used a footing on the jewelry itself so that it could maintain stability under the skin/tissue and allow the top to be interchanged with different designs or gems. Sean had recently released an instructional video on DVD that was received very well within the piercing industry.

At the Magic trade show, Vanessa asked Sean to meet in her booth, and they discussed the possibility of him designing one of these piercings for her company. They talked again on the phone the following week. As one of the pioneers of this new technique, she felt Sean would bring a sense of credibility to the piece.

As with any collaboration, Sean felt that his involvement needed to add value. Vanessa agreed to his terms right away, so the negotiation was the easy part. Sean agreed to design the new jewelry on one condition: he had to be in full control and sign off on the final design and specs. Once he felt comfortable with the design, he would grant a manufacturing license to Vanessa's company, and we would essentially become partners in this product as long as it was being made.

It took Sean about three weeks to pull together the final design. He emailed it to Vanessa and scheduled a call to go through the design together. She was excited by the design and felt her team could carry out Sean's ideas. He wanted to use the highest implant-grade titanium made in the U.S. Other than using a precious metal like gold or platinum, it was one of the most expensive ways to manufacture the piece, but by far the safest, she agreed. The two talked over timelines and agreed to a contract in theory, and we filed for a patent on the piece that week.

Vanessa saw the value in what Sean was bringing to her company and knew she was going to make money with the new product. But she was more excited about making her company stand out in her industry and delivering a great product to her clients. That is a sure sign of a great business owner: when they value innovation and creation ahead of simply making money. Vanessa gained our respect and admiration for that, and we remain friends to this day.

Within a few months, Vanessa delivered the first prototypes to us. Sean looked them over intently for a few days and then went ahead with implanting the first set of microdermal anchors in a volunteer at Club Tattoo (see Figure 12–3). He tracked the procedure and the client's healing meticulously, so he knew whether it was working

FIGURE **12-3** Healed Microdermal Anchor in Client by Sean

properly or if the design needed to be modified before Vanessa's company started mass-producing them.

Although the initial set of anchors were healing well, Sean felt like there could be a couple of minor design adjustments that that would make insertion and removal easier for the piercer. Sean requested those changes from Vanessa and her team. The changes were made, and Sean went through the same process with the new set of prototypes. This time no alterations were necessary, so Vanessa set her team in motion to manufacturing and marketing the new product.

It did not take long for our product to get noticed, and within six months we were clearly the leaders in the industry for this type of jewelry. It launched Metal Mafia into the next level of success and enhanced Sean's reputation and credibility within the industry. Within 18 months, the U.S. Patent Office granted a patent on the design (see Figure 12–4). This was a major achievement for us, and we are immensely proud of it.

FIGURE **12-4** Microdermal Anchor Patent

NARROW YOUR FOCUS TO GROW YOUR GLOBAL BRAND

Along with the industry success, the immediate financial gain was apparent. Between 2005 and 2020, the microdermal anchor sold more than a million units, generated more than $5 million in revenue, and helped take a groundbreaking procedure in the body piercing industry from a rebellious taboo to a mainstream fashion statement.

In the meantime, our internet presence had grown to place us in the top ten tattoo studios organically searched for on Google. That brought a lot of attention from international markets, as did our flagship studio in Las Vegas, which was an international travel destination.

With the global spotlight coming around more often, we were able to further develop the celebrity clientele that the studio was becoming known for; our celebrity partner Chester Bennington was constantly pushing the brand as well. This eventually brought us the collaboration deals we've talked about, as well as others with companies like Red Monkey, Caesars Entertainment, The Venetian Resort's Grand Canal Shoppes, and the Miracle Mile Shops.

These well-known brands had a distribution network that reached all over the globe, and by partnering with them, Club Tattoo gained not only a recognizable global presence but also instant credibility with people who never would have thought of a tattoo or piercing studio as a legitimate business.

However, the more successful we became through these partnerships, the more muddled our story got. At one point, there were literally too many facets of the company for us to describe them all to clients, let alone put them into a cohesive marketing package. Our marketing quickly became convoluted, and our messaging became confusing to our customers. We needed to take a time-out, take a fresh look at our mission statement, and reset our core brand messaging. We were so proud of everything that was going on (and with good reason!) that we started to forget what our company was really about.

In the end, we decided to pick one or two of the exciting things that were happening (such as our playing cards, shoes, or backpack line) and focus on telling that story and getting our clients interested in what the company was doing as a whole. However, we purposefully put all this into a secondary position, below our core offering of tattoos and piercings. By collaborating with these global brands, they were able to put together marketing campaigns that solely focused on the collaborative product we had done. The collaborations would of course sell the intended items for the companies, but the ancillary effect was to drive more traffic to our storefronts and create a stronger branding image for Club Tattoo. You can see some more examples of these partnerships in Figures 12–5, below, and 12–6, on page 136. We were a tattoo and piercing shop first, no matter what else was happening in our business, and we needed to make sure that our clients focused on that above anything else.

FIGURE **12-5** Red Monkey Hat collaboration with Club Tattoo

FIGURE **12-6** A Close Look at Club Tattoo Bicycle Cards

13

WHAT YOU KNOW CAN END UP BITING YOU

By 2011, Club Tattoo had become one of the most successful tattoo and piercing studios in the world. It had achieved worldwide fame and was quickly becoming one of the few iconic brands in the industry. Landlords from various properties around the world were starting to take notice of its flagship store inside Planet Hollywood Miracle Mile Shops in Las Vegas. We were generating approximately $3.8 million annually from that location alone.

Throughout Club Tattoo's business life span, Thora and I have relied on five essential characteristics to maintain its presence and success in each market:

1. *Location.* Choosing higher-traffic locations brought us more traffic. It usually came at a higher operating

cost as well, which eliminates many of your competitors from the same opportunities. In the case of choosing a storefront location, the location matters but comes with long list of questions that need to correlate directly with your specific business model (as we will talk in length about in this chapter). Traffic isn't the only consideration.

2. *Customer experience.* We strive to make our customers feel good about themselves, delivery quality product/work from our studios, and, just as importantly, make sure they understand that what we provide to them as an experience is far better than what our competitors offer. Everything from how the customer is greeted to where they are driven into the studios, the interactive items such as our touchscreen interface, the massive collection of quality gold and diamond body jewelry, our branded merchandise, and our follow up are all designed to make the entire customer journey a fun, enlightening, and cohesive experience.

3. *Marketing.* We take our marketing seriously and design entire campaigns for the purpose of not simply driving traffic but to build brand integrity and perception that we are at the very top of our industry and leading the way with lifestyle, safety, and innovation. The message of who you are and what you want people to perceive your brand to be must come through in your message.

4. *Traffic.* We have always tried to place our storefronts into the highest-traffic areas as possible, giving us the greatest chance for customer conversion. Though our stores are in super high-traffic areas, we use many other tools to drive even more traffic and make us a destination from the outset. In the modern era of being able to reach customers through different platforms, you can drive traffic through several ways such as Google, Instagram, Facebook, TikTok, Twitter, and many more. We are no longer simply reliant on walk/drive-by traffic for people to view our brand. Use the platforms that are available to drive the most traffic that will ultimately lead to

sales. Not all of these require massive investments; traffic can be driven through interaction on most, so engage and create your audience. It is also important not to confuse followers or impressions as dollars being generated, unless you have a solid correlation between them in your sales data.

5. *Brand consistency.* Throughout our business locations, there is a cohesive look, feel, and, most importantly, a fundamentally consistent operation. All of our storefronts arc unique in size and location, but our core functionalities are always the same. Our goal is to create and re-create the same customer experience for everyone who comes through our business. We have the luxury of selling a unique artistic experience in our business model so each customer gets their own unique experience; however, the way they are treated, their safety, and customer service should be relatively the same at each location. You can't both be the cheapest and the highest quality. Define what it is that your brand stands for and communicate that to your team and customer base. Make sure that your team is spreading the same message about your brand. What your brand stands for, the quality of your products, and the work environment for your staff all speak to your brand. Be sure that you are the ones directing what that brand message is, and keep it consistent so not only you know what it is your brand is and stands for but so does everyone else.

These were not the only things that made our company a success, but they are key elements to our journey as brand renegades—even when that journey exposed us to jeopardy. For us, that brand jeopardy became a factor during a time in Club Tattoo's history when we thought everything was aligned for success. As it turns out, one of our major success characteristics—location—ended up affecting the other four (customer experience, marketing, traffic, and brand consistency) and jeopardized our brand. In this chapter, we are going to focus on how these five elements all need to be in alignment in order for a brand to succeed and how we needed to ensure that alignment before our competitors beat us to new prime markets. Ultimately, this chapter is a cautionary tale about how when even one of these characteristics doesn't work (in this case, location), it can affect your brand choices and path forward. For us, it all started with location, and a famous one at that—San Francisco's Pier 39.

LOCATION, LOCATION, LOCATION

Sometime in 2010, we were contacted by one of the most famous properties in the United States about opening another flagship store in San Francisco. Pier 39 had become world-renowned, not only for its placement near the San Francisco Embarcadero, but also for its spectacular views of the Golden Gate Bridge and Alcatraz Island, among many other sights. It proudly boasted of its 80,000 daily visitors.

As with each of our locations, it all started with a meeting. As we've already told you, our motto is "Always take a meeting." You never know what is going to happen, what opportunities will arise, or who you will meet. We flew out to San Francisco to meet the board of directors and leasing team at Pier 39 in the winter of 2010. The entire staff greeted us with smiles and hugs, and the team leasing leader was incredibly inviting and warm. They genuinely wanted to see us on their property and continually expressed how much value we would add to their brand.

The leasing team leader led us on a tour of the property and gave us all the information we needed to decide whether to open a store in this market: daily traffic attendance, a competitive analysis of the area, the weather in San Francisco, and even the buying amounts and habits of the average customer.

Pier 39 had one of the most prestigious locations in the world that we could imagine: it was literally on the Pacific Ocean, in San Francisco, with a direct view of the Golden Gate Bridge out of the retail space we were looking to lease. As far as a location, it seemed like a no-brainer. This was an internationally known tourist mecca, and we would be prominently featured as part of the brand. One of the team members boasted about a recent survey the city of San Francisco had released stating that Pier 39 was the number-one tourist destination in the city, beating out the Golden Gate Bridge, Union Square, Little Italy, Alcatraz, and many other attractions. An average of 60,000 people a day came to the pier, adding up to a massive 22 million visitors annually. That was almost 20 percent more than we were seeing at our flagship studio on the Las Vegas Strip. It seemed impossible that we could improve on the immense amount of traffic we were seeing there. In fact, it seemed too good to be true.

In addition to the high volume of everyday traffic, the pier was frequently used in film shoots, so celebrity sightings were routine, and people often posted it as their location on social media, raising its profile even further.

The tenant mix at Pier 39 wasn't quite as appealing. We had learned over the years that potential customers' perception of our brand was affected by the companies around us. Think about it: If you were to see an unknown clothing store next to a Louis Vuitton, Tiffany, or Cartier store, what would you assume about that store? Most likely that it was an expensive, luxury, or elite brand, right?

We have all been to a high-end luxury mall before, with expensive and luxury stores clustered together. You're unlikely to find a discount retailer there. That is the result of a carefully planned tenant mix by the property managers. Likewise, we have been to a lower-end mall that hosts similar lower-end or discount brands—or it may have such an eclectic mix of stores that you can't identify the property's core brand. This latter case is caused by a bad tenant mix and poor organization by the property manager.

For Club Tattoo, we wanted to be at the higher mid-tier or lower-luxury side of the retail market. This is why our Las Vegas locations, for example, are at higher-end properties such as the Grand Canal Shoppes at The Venetian Resort, the Miracle Mile Shops at the Planet Hollywood Resort & Casino, and The LINQ Hotel + Experience. Take the Grand Canal Shoppes, for one—other retailers there include Burberry, Coach, Jimmy Choo, and Louis Vuitton. These luxury brands reinforce our high-end aesthetic and appeal to our desired demographic.

Pier 39's brands, on the other hand, were more along the line of Shula's restaurants, The Chart House, Fog Harbor Fish House, the Hard Rock Cafe, the Aquarium of the Bay, 7D Experience, and direct access to the bay tours. They were all solid mid-tier businesses, but we would definitely be at the higher end of the tenant mix. However, we felt most of these brands would still support our brand perception, and given the tremendous amount of foot traffic, all we needed to capture in a worst-case scenario was 0.5 percent of the daily traffic to do great. That seemed like a very reasonable assumption, given the data we had at the time.

IF SOMETHING DOESN'T FEEL RIGHT, IT USUALLY ISN'T

The stores we visited on our initial tour of the pier were welcoming and excited about Club Tattoo potentially opening a location there. They told us we would be an excellent fit for the pier, as many of the adults who visit wanted more experience-based shopping choices.

As we walked through the businesses on the pier, we couldn't help but notice that many of the retail stores were using old-fashioned cash registers and calculators to figure out the tax on individual items. This made no sense to us. How could businesses function with this much traffic and such out-of-date equipment? We weren't sure that we wanted to be adjacent to stores that did not offer the same customer experience for which our brand was known. Many of the stores even had hang tags with handwritten prices on their clothing items instead of scannable barcodes. It seemed clear these people had no idea how to run an efficient business. If they were actually making money this way, then we would be crushing it as soon as we opened our store. Perhaps our higher-end point-of-sale experience would elevate the game of the surrounding shops.

As we went back to the leasing offices, we grilled them about various issues: how their management team worked, their structure, and exactly what services the Pier provided for its tenants. The leasing team spoke only in generalities, but everything they said sounded good, and the staff's intentions came across as genuine. We were eager to open another amazing studio and further expand our brand's reach.

DIFFICULT NEGOTIATIONS OFTEN MEAN ROUGH SAILING AHEAD

During the lease negotiations that followed, I called our partner and friend Chester Bennington and asked him if he wanted to invest in another store location in San Francisco, just as he had done in the Las Vegas store location in 2009. After I gave him a brief rundown of what we wanted to do, Chester said he was in, and offered to invest $300,000. We eventually put up approximately $700,000 of our own money and took on an additional $1.1 million in debt in the form of an SBA loan. This was a huge risk for us at the time, but we felt we could make it work.

After nine months of lease negotiations, we finally came to an agreement. We had dealt with multimillion-dollar leases before and knew they took time to complete, but the Pier 39 legal team seemed to drag their feet over the simplest terms.

In hindsight, we should have walked away right then. We were stubborn, however, and we wanted to see the thing through. We signed a ten-year lease with Pier 39 in July 2012. The space we were leasing was about 3,400 square feet at a cost of about $23,000 per month, with a $3,000 marketing fee on top of that. Even after the difficult negotiations, we felt very positive about what we were doing and had an excellent game plan for opening the studio, hiring staff, marketing the location, and operating it from afar.

Looking back, the enormous red flags were already clear, but we were moving full steam ahead. As it turned out, the lease negotiations were only the first of the problems we were about to face in San Francisco.

SOME PROBLEMS CAN PUT YOU UNDERWATER—LITERALLY

During our lease negotiations, Thora had observed a large number of water pipes running through and around the ceiling in our proposed space that belonged to the drainage and water supply system of the restaurant upstairs from us, which was called Neptune's Café We were concerned that if one of the pipes leaked or broke, our space would be damaged or destroyed. We eventually negotiated a clause in our lease that if the pipes caused any damage, Neptune's Café would be responsible for all damages and must pay us directly. This eased our minds.

Once we signed the lease, we began the in-depth design process, which Thora usually handled. But what seemed to take two or three weeks in other cities was proving to take two to three months in San Francisco. The city officials were in no hurry to expedite anything for a small business like ours.

To make matters worse, since our business was located on the pier, we also had to report to a separate administrative board called the Bay Area Beautification Bureau. This board was supposed to try to uphold standards along the water's edge, but we found it to be one of the most corrupt and inept governmental agencies we have had to deal with on a regular basis.

Many of the bureau's fees made little to no sense or didn't improve the bay's businesses or city infrastructure. All we could see the fees doing was paying to employ more city officials. San Francisco was easily the most unfriendly city to small businesses that we had ever encountered. But we chalked these issues up to doing business in an unfamiliar city and figured that we would eventually learn our way around. But we had to wonder if this location was worth the risk. Was a prominent spot on Pier 39 going to pay off for our brand?

We had been working with our designers to build all the specialized millwork, cabinetry, and floor fixtures for several months before signing the final lease. This gave us a huge head start, so that all we would have left to do when we took possession of our space was a few plumbing and electrical issues, and then we could install our fixtures. On July 4, 2012, the pier called me (Sean) to set up a meeting to formally hand over the keys. I had taken our son Carston and my father, Kip, out to San Francisco for the holiday weekend, so when I met up with the rep to get the keys, I would be able to show them our new space.

That day, July 4, the pier was gearing up for a huge firework celebration, and the crowd was absolutely massive, adding to the excitement. We met the pier representative at the doors of the new space, directly in front of the world-famous sea lions. As soon as the representative opened the doors, we were hit with the stench of moldy seawater. We could see that the wood flooring throughout our space was bent and twisted; it had been severely damaged by water coming from somewhere in the ceiling and had clearly been rotting for a week or two.

I called Thora to tell her the situation, and the pier management told us they would fix the flooring and not to worry about it. We were grateful at the time because they appeared eager to help and we knew that we had written this into our lease for precisely this reason. It took approximately four weeks for the flooring to get repaired. It was a big job and it needed to be done right, so we were not pushing too hard to rush it.

But we didn't realize that we should have immediately given the keys back to the pier, because although they were fixing our floor, we were paying rent on a damaged and unusable space the whole time. Our new landlord was not operating in good faith. They simply wanted to start collecting rent as soon as possible. This was just another of many red flags to come when dealing with our new landlord. Not only that, but if we continued to have damage once the store opened, it would be detrimental to the customer experience and consistency we valued highly.

BUYER BEWARE WHEN IT COMES TO FEES

Once the flooring was finally fixed, the design build firm could get moving on the remainder of the electrical and plumbing and installation of the fixtures.

Although the building process was slower and much more difficult than we were used to, we were eventually able to open on

October 5, 2012, approximately 45 days past our original target date. The obstacles still seemed manageable at the time, and we weren't going to let a few setbacks discourage us.

It was evident by this point that our landlord was little more than a rent collector. Per the lease, we had to contribute approximately $3,000 per month into a marketing fund for the pier. However, the pier could use those funds however it chose. Not once did we find our brand integrated into any of the marketing the pier was doing, and that would be a constant battle for the next three years.

Within the first three months of our opening, we had another damaged water pipe from the building above, once again affecting our ability to maintain good traffic, market properly, and provide a consistent customer experience. We called the property management immediately and were told to work it out with Neptune's Café, as they were responsible for the damage, according to our lease. Neptune's told us to go away. They had no intention of paying for the damage and were content to let us sue them for the money.

The damage to the flooring was only a few thousand dollars this time, so we decided to handle it ourselves. The pipe problem continued to plague our business for the next three years, eventually totaling five major floods that caused more than $50,000 in damages.

THE TAX MAN ALWAYS, ALWAYS COMETH

As we got the studio up and running, we started to encounter other problems unique to our new location. The city of San Francisco had recently passed a new tax that we had not heard about until after we opened our doors. Apparently, many of the small businesses in the city had been avoiding paying their sales taxes for years, so the city decided to crack down by implementing a "gross use tax."

This is simply a tax based on the amount of revenue your company brings in, regardless of whether or not it is profitable. The tax was 1 percent of gross sales from every small business that grossed more than $1 million, and was in addition to the 7.5 percent sales tax that was already in place. Most of you can probably figure out how many tattoo and piercing studios in San Francisco made more than

$1 million in gross annual sales in 2013. Yes, that is correct, you win the grand prize. Only one studio in the entire city: Club Tattoo.

We received our first tax bill at the beginning of 2014, just after our first full year of sales in 2013 of $1.8 million. The tax bill was for $36,000. But that math didn't add up: 1 percent of $1.8 million is only $18,000. It seemed the city had decided that some businesses (including us) were a flight risk for not paying their taxes, so they wanted next year's gross use taxes in advance, based on the current year's numbers. So we had to pay $36,000 or get our licenses revoked and go out of business. We reluctantly paid it, but the writing was on the wall. This was starting to take a major toll on our morale, time, and sanity.

Do you remember when we took that tour of the pier and looked down our noses at the antiquated business practices of the other retail stores? We immediately jumped to the conclusion that they didn't know what they were doing. We were wrong. By using the old-style registers and not keeping their records on computers, they were rigging the system to avoid paying the taxes and fees based off their retail gross.

We thought we knew better, and it bit us in the ass.

PUT YOUR TRUST IN THE RIGHT PEOPLE

Keeping our studio staffed was as problematic as dealing with the city's tax codes. It seemed like we were going through employees every other week, and just getting them to show up on time was a major victory. The pier in general had a lackadaisical attitude of employment, and accountability was at the very top of things its work culture was lacking.

In 2014, we had an employee who had worked for us for several months. The employee had been trained by our senior staff and had signed an employment handbook acknowledging our processes, including treatment of other staff members, store closing procedures, and handling money.

One night the employee called to tell us the store had been robbed. After we made sure no one had been hurt and the police had been notified, we asked what had happened. They explained that they were closing out the cash drawer and turned their back for just a second when someone ran up, grabbed the money in the drawer, and quickly fled the store.

None of this sounded plausible, as we have strict guidelines on handling the cash drawers while closing, so Thora decided to watch the surveillance footage. The employee removed the cash drawer and set it on top of the counter while the store was still open and customers were milling about. They then walked away and into the office, leaving the drawer unattended, and one of the customers simply took all the money and left the studio. Several minutes later, the employee walks back out of the office and is clearly confused by the sight of the emptied drawer.

After reviewing the footage, the staff member finally admitted that what they did was wrong and entirely avoidable. We decided that they were no longer reliable or trustworthy enough to be employed by us, and terminated them.

This is where the city of San Francisco once again failed us. After several days, our former employee decided to bring legal action against Club Tattoo for wrongful termination. This is bound to happen eventually to any business owner. However, we had everything on film and a rock-solid employment handbook signed by the employee. We thought our case was a slam-dunk.

At the hearing, Thora showed the video and the handbook and explained what the employee had done wrong. Perry Mason would have been proud. The former employee made no argument about why they were wrongfully terminated, only that they did not feel it was right.

It took approximately ten minutes for the labor board to rule that we had wrongfully terminated the employee based on their "normal negligence." In other words, they felt the employee should not have been terminated for leaving cash out on a counter because they were not willfully trying to hurt the company. Although it was made clear that we did nothing illegal by firing the employee, they still qualified for an unemployment claim. Although it wasn't a legal ruling against us, it still stung to hear the government's justification for granting our former employee's claim.

KNOW WHEN TO GET OFF YOUR ASS AND GET OUT

By the following year, business had started to pick up, although it would never reach our original projections or ever come close to our expectations. We were losing about $60,000 per year just operating the business. We were not spending enough time with our children, we were feeling disconnected from our family unit, and none of it was worth it anymore. Many of our five brand characteristics had been affected by moving forward with the Pier 39 store, and it showed. Our location was not working out the way we hoped, and it was affecting customer experience, our ability to properly market the brand, how much traffic we got, and our overall brand consistency.

In January 2015, we received yet another call from one of our staff members stating that there had been a major flood from the restaurant above when they arrived at work. There had been thousands of dollars in damaged merchandise as well as damage to our ceiling, electrical fixtures, and jewelry cases. The worst part of this specific flood was that it had ruined a large part of our $60,000 solid wood floor directly at the entrance. The wood planks started cupping and pulling up, and it quickly became a tripping hazard for our staff and clients.

We approached the Neptune's Café management about the damage, who assured us that it would be handled and paid for within a month. This was the fifth time they had caused flooding damage, and they had never paid us before. A month came and went, and sure enough, they blew us off. Once again, we had to make the decision between repairing the floor, which would have cost us roughly $20,000 (plus the costs of shutting down the store for a week), or filing legal action against the restaurant and the pier while our store remained in disrepair.

As we looked into litigation, we learned some new information that brought everything into focus: Neptune's Café was actually owned by several of the same people who owned Pier 39. Without question this was a major conflict of interest and put us in a difficult situation.

We had hit our breaking point; enough was enough. Sean flew out to San Francisco for an emergency meeting with our landlord and explained that we were going to exercise a clause in our lease to leave at the end of the year. We no longer trusted the landlord, as they had wiggled around just about every fiduciary responsibility they had to us, including enforcing the lease's ceiling leak provisions that had damaged so much of our store fixtures and property. The pier's management team was stunned and tried to talk us out of leaving, assuring us that things would get better if we only held on for a little longer.

Club Tattoo San Francisco could have stayed open, but our landlord was one of the worst we had ever encountered, and there were sure to be major issues with the ceiling moving forward. Our escape clause was only good for the first three years of our lease. We decided that it was better to take the loss and put our energy and focus where it would have the most impact on our company as a whole. We had had enough of Pier 39 and San Francisco at that point, and just wanted out of the lease, our store, and the city altogether.

Over the next few months, we put together a financial plan for redistributing our nearly $1 million debt and renegotiating our SBA loan so we didn't take a hit on our credit or lose the collateral we had put up. We had to put up three of our major housing assets to guarantee the SBA loan, and we did not want to lose our initial cash investment and our physical assets.

It was heartbreaking to finally close the location, but it was the right decision. In our final nine months, the store grossed nearly $1.6 million and we still lost about $60,000 that year. We were beginning to feel like we were treading water. Our other locations—and, most important, our children—were the real losers in all this, as our time was soaked up by a project that was paying no dividends, both metaphorically and literally. Once we closed the doors to our Pier 39 store in October 2015, the weight finally lifted from our shoulders and we could try to repair the damage that had been done on many fronts.

Everything we "knew" about our company in 2011 caused us to make one of the biggest mistakes in our entrepreneurial existence. We ended up losing more than $2 million and four years on that store. We nearly crumbled under the weight of the failure, but our resolve to push through and overcome led us out of the chaos and on to much bigger successes. Looking back, we should have done more due diligence and looked further into some of the underlying issues we were seeing and the red flags that were waving in our faces before we signed that lease. Fortunately, we worked harder in other areas and were able to pay off the entire loan by 2020.

CHAPTER

14

F*!% IT.
DO IT ANYWAY.

"Y ou can't do that!" This has been said so frequently to us that it has become a challenge. The words "you can't" are merely someone else's internalized fear being projected onto you. They are putting their insecurities onto you, either to make themselves either feel superior to you or to make themselves feel better about the things they believe they cannot accomplish. In either case, use these five simple words to prove to yourself that they are wrong: *Fuck it. Do it anyway*. Standing around and waiting for something to happen is not how we are wired. We need to create and capitalize on the opportunities that present themselves. We love coming up with ideas, but an idea without action is simply a fantasy or an illusion. In this chapter, we'll walk you through our "Fuck

It. Do It Anyway" moments and how they helped us re-envision and reframe our brand for the long run.

FIRST IMPRESSIONS MAY NOT TELL THE WHOLE STORY

During our time at Pier 39, we were continually courted by other properties around the world, but we had become wary of jumping into a bad decision again and didn't want to repeat our mistake in San Francisco. Our agent in Las Vegas, Frank Volk, had been pitching several of the nicer resort properties in hopes of luring us into a relationship with Caesars Entertainment. We had been offered retail locations at Bally's Las Vegas Hotel and Casino, the Grand Bazaar Shops, The Cosmopolitan, Treasure Island, Harrah's in New Orleans, The Tropicana in Atlantic City, and more.

One day in 2014, Frank asked us to come to Vegas and meet with one of Caesars' representatives to look at a property called The Quad. As we've said, we always take a meeting, so we flew up in a few days. As we arrived at the property, we immediately knew it wasn't a good fit. There's no way to describe it other than as a dump. We felt we were wasting our time being shown around the dirty casino with its nasty carpet and overwhelming smell of cigar smoke. We wanted nothing to do with it, so at the end of the tour we exchanged pleasantries and went home.

Frank called us a few weeks later to discuss The Quad. We were blatantly honest with him and told him we were surprised he would even show us that property, as it clearly was not a good brand match for Club Tattoo. We had always positioned ourselves as a high-end or high-midtier property. It wouldn't make any sense for us to take a retail location in a rundown property like that one.

Frank calmed us down and explained that The Quad had been purchased by Caesars, which had committed itself to redeveloping the entire property: remodeling the rooms, completely re-leasing their retail offering and tenant mix, and redesigning the casino from top to bottom. It was also building a giant observation wheel called the High Roller. Measuring 550 feet in diameter, the High Roller would eclipse both the London Eye and the Singapore Flyer observation wheels. It was going to face north and south parallel to Las Vegas Boulevard but pushed back about 1,500 feet from the strip, creating a large walking area and retail environment for the Las Vegas Boulevard walking visitors.

The High Roller wheel would take approximately 30 minutes to complete one full revolution and would feature 28 glass-enclosed cabins, with broad views of Las Vegas and the Strip. Each spherical cabin would hold up to 40 people, with benches on either side of the cabin featuring a private bartender, and plenty of floor space in between. It was going to be truly amazing.

The opening of the new hotel was scheduled for October 30, 2014. The new hotel would match the vibe of the promenade: sexy, modern, chic, and in close proximity to retailers and the 550-foot-tall High Roller. The property had been designed by architect Elkus Manfredi, and the new restaurant and bar offerings would include widely popular Guy Fieri's Vegas Kitchen & Bar, Hash House A Go Go, Off the Strip, a sexy Mexican food concept called Chayo, and Tag Lounge and Bar. The hotel would house 2,252 rooms and be renamed The LINQ Hotel + Experience (shown in Figure 14–1 below).

FIGURE 14-1 The LINQ Hotel + Experience

Frank sent over some of the renderings of what the property was going to look like, along with the committed investment layout from Caesars. They were going to invest more than $550 million into the property and into bringing up the overall standard and perception of the hotel. Once we looked over the plans and understood their direction, we decided to take a closer look and flew out several times to get a better feel for the property before making our decision.

PLACING OUR BETS ON THE LINQ

After months of going over the numbers, we decided to sign a ten-year lease with The LINQ. The two of us had to seriously look at our financial obligations and make sure that we could not only withstand the new store expenditure but also take on the possibility of it not generating money right out of the gate. At the time, we were still having issues with our San Francisco location, and it was looking increasingly likely that we would have to close it.

Once again, we reached out to our partner Chester and asked if he wanted to be involved in the newest location. We knew he might very well not be interested, given the current state of the market and the situation with our San Francisco studio, so we were prepared to finance the new studio entirely with our own money. But no sooner had we finished our sales pitch than he responded with a quick, "Absolutely. I would love to be involved."

The LINQ location (see Figure 14–2 on page 157) would be an experiment for us. The entire store was only going to be approximately 1,100 square feet, which was much smaller than our other stores. But a smaller store meant inherently less risk, and if it did not prove to be profitable, our other Las Vegas location could offset some of the losses. We had our fingers crossed, however, that this would not be the case, and we tried to mitigate every possibility of failure in planning for the new store.

We built the store with a 100 percent cash investment. The entire studio was built and stocked on a budget of less than $500,000, with Chester chipping in $150,000, and a little more

FIGURE **14-2** Thora and Sean with the Construction and Design Crew at The LINQ Club Tattoo Location

than $330,000 provided by us. This was an amazing feat, as we had learned very quickly on our first build in Las Vegas that dealing with local labor was two to three times more expensive than in other markets. We had learned valuable lessons from our San Francisco problems as well, managing to trim costs prior to the permitting stage and taking as few field revisions to our construction as possible.

In less than 90 days, we had the entire store completed, and it looked phenomenal. With our existing reputation, it proved quite easy to staff the new studio with talented tattoo artists and body piercers. We had more than 120 applicants and interviewed nearly 60 of them for only 11 positions. We put together a marketing plan that we integrated with our existing Las Vegas marketing and had it up and running during the entire construction process in order to build up local buzz about the upcoming grand opening.

THE GAMBLE PAYS OFF

We opened The LINQ location of Club Tattoo on March 1, 2015 (see Figures 14–3 and 14–4 below), and received an enormous amount of positive feedback. We were busy from open to close on our first day, and after the stress we had been under, it was a huge relief. It started to make money from the first month of being open, just as its sister store at Planet Hollywood Miracle Mile had done. It

FIGURE **14-3** Club Tattoo Storefront at The LINQ Hotel + Experience

FIGURE **14-4** Inside the Club Tattoo at The LINQ Hotel + Experience

was a much-needed confidence booster to be reminded that we had a great concept and we did know what we were doing.

The LINQ and Caesars' management teams were overwhelmingly happy with our store and would bring potential tenants inside to boast about how successful we were at their property. Within the first two years of The LINQ's location opening its doors, we had earned our entire investment back and made an immediate impact in the local tattoo and piercing scene. It was apparent that none of our competitors in the Las Vegas market were going to make much of an impact on our market share. Chester was exceptionally happy with the return on his investment, and we felt immensely proud that we were creating such a successful, meaningful, and profitable company.

The icing on the cake was our new landlord. Unlike the poor experience we had had with the management at Pier 39, The LINQ took an active role in making sure they brought value to their tenants by including us in their marketing, on-property brand messages, and overall inclusion in their public image. We had a partner in The LINQ, just as we had with the Miracle Mile Shops, which both understood that Club Tattoo had added value to their properties.

BUILDING OUR GLOBAL BRAND

As the Club Tattoo brand surged regionally thanks to its store locations, our global reach was much greater than we might have expected. This was primarily due to the licensing and collaboration deals we had put together over the previous ten years. We were receiving emails and calls from properties all over the world, from London to Melbourne, Australia, wanting our brand to open more high-end stores. But since we were still footing the bill to open each store location, our capacity to grow was confined to how much cash flow we had at the time.

It seemed that every couple of years, we had been opening a new studio, and all our available cash was getting sucked up into each new location. All the studios were giving us a return on our investment, but each one still took on average two to five years to pay us back in full. Multiply that over four locations, and that was a lot of money invested that we were waiting to see a return on. We were starting to see how risky it was to continue funding stores with our own cash.

Just about the time that we started realizing our cash-flow crisis, we received a call from a soft-spoken woman named Gina. She happened to call on the day we were opening our LINQ studio, when our cell phones were ringing a hundred times a day and we had to answer every call.

Gina explained that she wanted to meet and discuss the possibility of opening a studio inside the new Harley-Davidson dealership in North Scottsdale in the upcoming six months. Immediately Sean wanted to say no, but our "always take a meeting" rule still applied, so he agreed and then hung up.

When he told Thora about it, she looked at him with fright in her eyes and said, "Absolutely not. No fucking way."

We had just spent nine months getting our newest studio ready to open and had worked 10 to 14 hours a day for the past two weeks. We were both beat, and the thought of doing it all over again was not very appealing. Still, we would at least listen to the proposal before we politely turned it down.

We met the Harley-Davidson team for lunch at a nice restaurant in North Scottsdale. Gina explained that their dealership was to be the most luxurious and largest Harley-Davidson dealership in the world, with more than 150,000 square feet of retail space. It would have a tattoo shop, a wedding chapel, a movie theater, and much more, and they wanted Club Tattoo to be part of it.

It sounded exciting, but we really didn't want to open another studio, and we weren't sure Harley was a good brand fit for Club Tattoo. We had always assumed that most Harley riders were older and had less discretionary income than our ideal demographic.

Gina politely informed us that we had not done our research: According to *Cyril Huze Post*, the number-one magazine for custom motorcycle news, "Harley is the USA market leader among riders ages 18 to 34, as well as women, African Americans, and Hispanics.

As a matter of fact, the average age for Harley riders in the United States was going down each year." The demographic still seemed a little older than what we were hoping for, but their discretionary income was far greater than our current average clients.

But in the end, we politely declined, telling them we did not think it was for us and we were going to pass on the opportunity. Gina looked at us and very seriously said, "I don't think you understand. 'No' is not an answer [owner Bob Parsons] will accept."

We were immediately offended, as if a mafia capo had just threatened us. That was straight out of a movie, but she was serious. She could see that we were upset, but as the situation calmed down, she explained about Bob Parsons.

He was the founder of internet web hosting company GoDaddy and one of the richest people in the U.S., with a net worth of approximately $3 billion. He was also an avid motorcycle rider who owned Harley-Davidson dealerships in three states. His pitch was simple: he wanted to build the most amazing Harley-Davidson dealership in history, no matter how much it cost him or what he had to do to get it done, and that included getting us onboard. Gina asked if we would be willing to open a studio in their new dealership if they took on all the costs associated with building it. They in turn would give us any lease terms we felt were fair on a simple one-sheet contract.

At this point in our careers, our contracts were usually 100 pages long and always included a hundred hours of attorney's fees to decipher them. They were going to build out the entire studio to our specs, no cutting corners, and we did not have to pay a dime? The icing on the cake was that they included rent as a percentage of sales, due 30 days in arrears. This deal sounded too good to be true, but it was certainly too good to pass up.

Guys like Bob Parsons don't have time for "no." They want something done and they want it done yesterday, so they are usually willing to pay a premium for it. We finally agreed to the terms, but the dealership was scheduled to open in four months, so we had to start designing the studio fast.

CLICKING WITH A PARTNER: THE BEST KIND OF MAGIC

Within a week or so, Thora began working with the head architect and designers for the dealership. Our space was the smallest studio we had ever opened—only 777 square feet in total—but it turned out beautifully and kept the look and feel of the Club Tattoo brand, even though it was part of the Harley-Davidson dealership. It was important to us that our brand integrity wasn't compromised in the new studio, since we had spent years by this point establishing our look and feel for our customers.

When we did finally meet with Bob Parsons, we found him to be one of the more genuine people we have ever done business with. He was a little irritated with us at first for not jumping on his opportunity, which he felt was a "no-brainer," but Sean was honest with him about our reasoning. We hit it off and developed a great working relationship, and he has since become a friend. He once told us that our attitude reminds him of when he was young and didn't stop at the first sign of trouble. Although he has far greater resources than we do, we share the same mindset of getting things done, no matter what the obstacles. It was truly an honor to meet and get to know a successful, driven entrepreneur and visionary like Bob Parsons. It was great to do business with him and even greater to hear him say to another staff member:

> The reason we chose doing business with Sean and Thora at Club Tattoo was because they were the very best in their industry. I wanted the best, and that's what I sent my team after.

Bob Parsons' Harley-Davidson dealership, complete with Club Tattoo, opened in October 2015 to the sound of thunderous applause and rumbling motorcycles. At the grand opening event, we had the honor of meeting Arizona Governor Doug Ducey and then-Maricopa County Sheriff Joe Arpaio, along with several well-known musicians and other entertainers. Thousands of people showed up, and virtually everyone was impressed, both with the dealership and with Club Tattoo.

Our brand grew even stronger with our affiliation with Harley-Davidson. Club Tattoo keeps growing larger and getting stronger as a brand, and with the momentum we have built over the past 20-plus years, we plan on opening many more all over the globe.

BACK TO THE STRIP

In February 2019, we were again in the market to open another location in a higher-end property on the Las Vegas Strip. We had been taking meetings at several casinos while trying to make sure that we chose an upscale property that would improve our portfolio and brand perception. It would take nearly seven months to negotiate our newest studio location.

The Venetian and the Palazzo are among the finest hotels and casinos in Las Vegas, if not the country. They have one of the most successful malls in the world running through both hotels and connecting them in the middle, called the Grand Canal Shoppes. They opened in 1999 and have truly brought an upscale experience to the center of the Las Vegas Strip.

The motif of the resort is loosely based on the city of Venice. It has re-created the beautiful ceiling paintings of the Venetian palaces throughout the property. It even has a canal offering gondola rides with gondoliers who sing, running daily through the middle of the property to give it that authentic feeling (or as much authenticity as you can get in Vegas!).

The Venetian (shown in Figure 14–5 on page 164) is also home to one of the world's most renowned and best nightclubs, Tao. Tao has been in business since 2005 and quickly became the top nightclub in the city. The studio location that we had our eye on was literally right out in front of Tao.

We had been to Tao several times, stayed at the Venetian and Palazzo, and shopped in the Grand Canal Shoppes. We loved the property and knew it would be a perfect fit for Club Tattoo, so we starting working on our financial pro formas to see the vision become a reality.

FIGURE **14-5** The Venetian and Palazzo Hotel and Casino, Las Vegas

After we went through our design ideas and layout, we realized it would cost nearly $800,000 to open. That was a lot more than we had hoped, and we had become very debt-shy after our San Francisco studio closed. We were still paying off the debt from that studio, and the pain of that failure had not quite dissipated, so we were hoping to self-fund the new studio. We organized our financial portfolio and made the necessary adjustments to fund the entire store ourselves, without taking on any partners or debt. The recent loss of our friend and partner Chester had taken a large toll on us, and we didn't want to convolute our ownership any further at this point.

In October 2019, we finally opened the doors to Club Tattoo at the Venetian Grand Canal Shoppes (shown in Figure 14–6 on page 165), and it was an immediate success.

Sometimes, things can truly fall in your lap and you have to be prepared to act and take massive action in order to take full advantage of the opportunity that is placed in front of you. Sometimes luck can present itself as an opportunity. However, you can only take advantage of that luck and become "lucky" if you are prepared to take advantage of the opportunity by taking action.

There were many times when opportunities came our way and we could have said, "We are too busy for this at the moment," or

FIGURE **14-6** Club Tattoo at the Venetian Grand Canal Shoppes

shrugged it off as an opportunity that will come again. We felt that certain opportunities were too good to pass up. Although we may have been extremely busy during those moments or financially spread too thin, we took calculated risks in order to expand and grow our brand.

It didn't always work out the way we planned as we have had many failures within our organization. But more often than not, it was worth the risk, and our company grew as a result. As we would come to find out very quickly, it isn't just the risk of what you are trying to accomplish that can have disastrous consequences. As an entrepreneur, sometimes it doesn't matter how good your business model is. Not everything is in your control.

CHAPTER

15

WHEN THE BUSINESS WORLD STOPPED

We thought we were prepared for anything. We really did. If you had asked us in January 2019 if we thought we could ever go out of business, our answer would have been a resounding "Not a chance." In fact, if we had written this book in any other year, our perspective might vary, but it would pale in comparison to the book we would write in 2020. In this chapter, we're taking a pause in our story (much like the sudden pause we all experienced in 2020) to share the story of how the pandemic affected (and is still affecting) our business and brand.

MARCH 2020: A GRINDING HALT

As we lay in bed on the evening of March 17 (Thora's birthday), we were getting notifications that the casinos in

Las Vegas were shutting down the next day, and we had to secure our stores and be out by 5 P.M. We were staring at each other in helplessness and fear, almost certainly a new emotion for both of us. Never before in our business lives had we known this type of uncertainty, and it would take nearly everything we had before we were sure our business would survive.

There was no timeline for reopening, and employees by the tens of thousands rushed to the unemployment line. We started to understand that the economic impact was going to be severe and we needed to formulate a strategy just to survive.

We had been watching the news at our home near Phoenix. It was telling stories of the newest virus to hit the planet—Covid-19—and discussing the immediate prognosis for the United States and the rest of the world. They were saying that if the country didn't immediately close down, we were possibly looking at millions of people dying in a pandemic, something we haven't seen since the flu pandemic of 1918 (which killed approximately 60 million people worldwide).

This seemed inconceivable as report after report hit the airwaves. The more we watched, the more bad news poured in. The president came on the news soon and various public officials started calling for shutdowns in some of the largest cities, like New York and Los Angeles.

MAKING HARD DECISIONS

In the coming days, we were forced to close all six Club Tattoo studios in Las Vegas and Arizona. Initially the states' governors implied it might be for about two to three weeks, so that we could "flatten the curve" of the infection rate. They had little data to go on, but they were hopeful that business closures were a temporary inconvenience that wouldn't have a huge impact over the long run. Little did we know that some of our businesses would be closed for three or more months and that we would lose millions of dollars in revenue.

As the days went on, we were getting reports that our properties in Las Vegas were posting signs of indefinite closure. This was disconcerting, as our landlords there were not returning our phone calls. (In all fairness, we are sure they had their hands full at the time.)

We did not understand the full scope of what was about to happen. No one could see the devastation that was about to happen around the world and in our country. But we could not help thinking about our businesses that we had worked so hard to make successful. What would happen to our staff if we had to close? What was going to happen to us? The stress was beginning to mount.

LOOKING FOR A LIFE RAFT

President Trump announced that he was working on getting a new law through Congress called the Payroll Protection Program (PPP) that would be available to all businesses with less than 500 employees. It was meant to help any small business that was struggling during the shutdown keep their employees so that they did not have to fire them, furlough them, or lay them off. We believed help was on the way. Our bank (Chase) assured us we would be eligible to apply and offered us some guidance on how to fill out the applications for the loan. Sean worked diligently with our accountant to make sure we had all the paperwork in order.

We had already decided not to lay off any of our staff—more than 100 people—and were paying them out of our own pocket. We thought this would only last a few weeks and that the government would come to our aid. We endured our first, second, and third payroll periods this way, and it was frighteningly obvious we could not sustain it without help.

We had already used more than $200,000 of our own money to fund our payroll, but it looked as if the PPP help was finally on the way. We knew that the loan amounts were going to be hefty, but at the end of the day our staff would be safe from evictions and could afford to put food on their table during the crisis.

GETTING IN LINE FOR PPP

When the start time for the PPP applications came, we were ready. Sean was on his computer, and when Chase opened their portal for submissions. Sean had them uploaded and submitted in less than five minutes. However, they stayed in limbo on the Chase portal, and within minutes we received a message that Chase was no longer taking submissions and the PPP funds had all been given out.

The only way this could have happened was through preferential treatment by the banks toward certain companies. But that is neither here nor there. What we had counted on went up in smoke, and panic started to set in. We had substantial savings, but it was disappearing fast under the pressures of making payroll, and without help, we were headed for insolvency fast.

The following day, our personal business banker called us to assure us that they did everything they could to help us and told us not to worry, that in the coming weeks another program would be available, and he would try to get us in that line as soon as possible. Maybe he actually believed that, but it seemed the banks had cut back-room deals rather than the funding going out to regular small businesses as intended. Weeks and even months later these assumptions would be proven true by reports of large businesses that did not meet the criteria receiving these loans rather than small businesses that did meet the loan requirements.

Stories continue to emerge of blatant corruption, favoritism, and manipulation between the federal government and the banks, but we had to push through regardless. One of the first rules you learn as an entrepreneur is that life isn't fair, so get over it and keep going.

Congress started to get massive pushback in the coming weeks when they decided to take a vacation in the middle of this storm we were enduring. They simply did not understand what was happening to the rest of the country. We need to give credit where credit is due, however, and the president and Congress realized the initial PPP fund was falling way short of meeting the country's needs. So they drew up a larger, more inclusive bill that would go to the small businesses that had missed out on the first round of funding.

Meanwhile, we were getting down to the bare bones of our bank accounts. We had spent more than $300,000 of our own money on payroll at this point and had decided we would have to lay off our entire staff as of April 30. Sean wanted to wait until May 1 before notifying the staff. The stress of having to lay off our entire team was taking its toll, and we were hoping for any kind of positive news to delay what we thought might be the inevitable. This way we could hope for something to change or get more information as to when we might be able to reopen, thus softening the blow of the layoffs. We knew if we used up all our cash reserves on payroll, we would not have enough to restart the businesses when the time eventually came to reopen.

MAKING TOUGH BUT NECESSARY DECISIONS

After we got over our initial anger about the decisions we were being forced to make, we came to an agreement: We were not going to let the world shut us down. We had worked too hard to create something special, and we could not simply give up and close our doors.

We still had some money in our savings, but it wasn't enough to keep everyone on staff for the foreseeable future, so we decided instead to invest in our company, so that when we reopened, our staff could come back to a better and safer work environment.

We decided to spend all but some reserve capital on remodeling and improving our stores, bringing them up to a health standard that would be above the rest of the field once the pandemic subsided and businesses were able to reopen. We invested in things like new flooring and new paint, but more importantly things like industrial HEPA filtration systems and touchless HEPA-filtrated Dyson hand dryers.

The morning of May 1 came, and as we woke up around 6 A.M., a feeling of absolute dread overcame us. We knew what we had to do; neither of us wanted it to happen, but we were out of options. We had been faced with complicated staffing choices in the past, but never a mass group layoff to save our company. It felt like choosing between them and us, and it was gut-wrenching.

Not much makes you cry after 25 years in business, but it felt like Thora had cried at least once a day for the past ten weeks.

Wiping away the tears, taking a deep breath, and saying, "Fuck this, what's next? Let's do this!" became a ritual every time the emotional flooding happened. Inaction was not an option—or even a consideration.

Sean shouldered his emotions quietly while trying to support Thora and spending hours and hours looking for help. The morning of May 1, Sean got on his phone to check our bank accounts, and we had finally received the PPP funding from the government. The restrictions on the money had changed, but at least we could pay our staff and not lay them off for the time being. There was life again in our company, and we knew (through many spreadsheets and calculations) we could last another two months before we had to make tough decisions again.

The government and Chase Bank came through for us in a time of crisis, and because of the way we managed our company, we were in a position to take advantage of the help that was being offered. Knowing exactly what our necessary expenses were in order to survive was a helpful tool throughout the entire process; we could have easily misallocated the funds and not been eligible for loan forgiveness by the federal government. Many of the businesses in our industry had to lay off their entire teams, and as far as we know, we may be one of the only tattoo and piercing studios that was able to pay their entire staff during the crisis.

THE BILLS DON'T STOP, EVEN WHEN THE WORLD DOES

After a few months of the shutdown, we started to see signs that it might be coming to an end. Unfortunately, we still had massive issues, including insurance companies that refused to pay business interruption claims and landlords that wanted us to pay full rent during the shutdown. Under normal circumstances, most businesses could afford to pay their rent for several months without being crushed. However, the rent structure in Las Vegas is a little different.

To help you understand the scale of the problem, the rent on our Planet Hollywood Miracle Mile store is $45,000 per month—ten times higher than the rent on our Arizona stores. After four months of being closed, just one store's rent debt would be nearly $200,000—and keep in mind we have three stores inside high-profile Las Vegas casinos, all of which were shut down. This was going to require an entirely different set of negotiating tools, or our rent debt could wipe out all three stores in Las Vegas. Luckily, our landlords were all understanding and knew that the entire commercial leasing market had been flipped upside down by the pandemic. We were eventually able to negotiate our leases with each landlord and come to a reasonable solution. Our landlords could have refused, but they saw the value that our studios brought to their properties and wanted us to stay open.

As time went on, we completed the store remodels, kept our staff on payroll, and geared up to reopen in June, but we did not know what to expect. Would the public be terrified to travel outside their homes? Would they be fearful of stepping into retail establishments? Would they spend money like they used to? We simply did not know, and we were worried that despite all our effort and sacrifice, we might end up failing anyway.

We knew from our past experience that we had to trust our instincts and keep our company's mission in mind of creating an atmosphere that made people feel safe and comfortable while still focusing on our main concept: art and expression. We were able to achieve this by believing in each other throughout the process. There were certainly moments of strife, uncertainty, and disagreements, but ultimately, we survived because we trusted each other as partners.

As the dust settled and our Arizona studios were permitted to reopen in June, business started off strong and strengthened our belief that we could succeed even in the worst circumstances. Our Las Vegas stores were permitted to reopen later in June, and although they started slower and are clearly not going to drive the company's revenue, as they did prior to the covid pandemic, it looks like we are on a sustainable path toward a successful business model in the near future.

CHAPTER

16

CREATE AN EXIT STRATEGY

ometimes, your business will have to pivot to an exit strategy either for the entire brand or for individual partners. Sometimes, that pivot involves a partner leaving the relationship or, sadly, passing away. We had to deal with this when our partner Chester Bennington passed away unexpectedly on July 20, 2017. When he died, his estate technically became our new business "partner." We never met any of the people involved in managing his estate before his death, other than his wife. We knew her personally, of course, but had never discussed business with her. The estate managers didn't know our business or anything else about us. This was an unforeseen and unintended consequence.

We set up our partnership agreement in 2004, which lacked an exit strategy for the event of a business partner's death. After Chester's passing, we never created any agreement without exit strategies and contingency plans again.

With this partnership, because we did not have a good exit plan, we had to speak with his estate for anything we wanted to do differently or change at that location. The estate gets profits from any sale, too, which is fair under the circumstances.

THORA: *Nobody wants to think about what happens when I die, or he dies. But if we were not married, Sean wouldn't want my kids or my husband to become his new business partner, because any other family members probably would not care or know anything about the business. This adds a layer of difficulty that is not necessary or desirable. All they know is they are holding on to one last part of their loved one—and there's money involved. It's an uncomfortable topic, to say the least, and nobody wants to be unkind or unfair to anyone involved, so it's better to plan prior to something like this happening.*

When taking on business partners, you should plan out and prepare for business growth strategies, just as you would with your exit strategy. For instance, if you're talking about expanding the business, when might you want to take on a new partner? What are the partnership buy-in and buy-out options? But the first question you should ask yourself is "Why do I want or need a partner?" You may be surprised at your answer and decide to change your approach.

When planning your exit from your company, make sure you are ready to sell when the timing is right to pursue your business's highest value. Sell on your terms, when and how you want. Just like in the stock market, the idea is to sell your asset at its highest value and hold it when the market is soft or undervalued. You most likely spent many years developing your company. Don't sell when you don't have to—or, worse yet, when you aren't ready to sell. The reason you started your business in the first place was to do something different or create something great on your own. Don't leave until you're ready, but be sure you have worked out a plan for when that time arrives. In this chapter, we'll share our thoughts about how we have planned our own exit strategy. And heads-up: we're doing this in an interview style so you can see our individual perspectives and contributions to this conversation.

A GOOD EXIT STARTS WITH A STRONG PLAN

We learned in math class that the shortest distance between two points is a straight line. Well, that may work on paper, but life hardly ever happens the way we think it will. Even when we follow the advice of people who claim to be smarter or more experienced, what worked for them may not work for us.

When "life happens," combined with poor or blurred communication, the results can be disastrous to a professional or personal partnership. Research and experience show that the more planning and communication involved in a partnership, the higher the success rate.

Even if the business partnership or marriage cannot be saved, it is a lot less complicated, messy, and painful if there is an exit strategy already in place. We can't think or make good choices when emotions are involved in emergencies or in response to unexpected situations. Two years ago, we would have laughed at someone telling us a pandemic would close all our businesses down for three or more months, but it happened. Thankfully, we were in a position to survive and eventually even thrive, through saving and making sure that our business ran above board by paying our taxes and keeping our debt in reasonable check

Think about it. There are contingency plans built into almost everything we do and everywhere we go. Hotels, schools, and stadiums have exit plans in case of severe weather or fire. On an airplane, the flight attendants explain various exit strategies by asking us to locate the closest emergency exits, instructing us on how to use the slides or floatation devices, and explaining how to use the oxygen masks in case the cabin loses air pressure.

Thinking about all the possible scenarios involved in creating an exit strategy for your business or personal life is hard. It is uncomfortable and emotional. For example, a will is an exit strategy for your life. Not many people want to talk about what will happen to their family, their belongings, or their business after they have died. But having a will makes the process easier for the people left behind when they are in the middle of a drastic emotional change.

> SEAN: *For an exit strategy to be possible, you have to understand yourself and define your goals. You must be contented with your professional and personal relationships. Then you must understand that your business is a real, viable, sellable product. These are all basic levels of clarity you need before you can talk about and create a usable exit strategy. Otherwise, it is going to be the same basic exit strategy as everyone else's. Lack of clarity leads to basic goals such as "Save up enough money to retire." That is an exit strategy; it's just not the fastest, most definable one, because it relies on the answers to such questions as "How many more years are you going to work?"*

> *Talking about or implementing an exit strategy wasn't something I wanted to do when I first opened the company or when Thora and I were first married in 1998. Thora joined the company full time in 2001 when we expanded from the original location. When I thought about the need for any kind of exit strategy, it brought up feelings of anxiety, uncertainty, and anger. I didn't want to think much about the future.*

But Sean knew he had to think about the future, especially in terms of the legacy of Club Tattoo. And he knew that meant strengthening his partnership with Thora.

STRONG PARTNERSHIP, STRONG STRATEGY

> SEAN: *At the time, I felt it was my business, and I was clear about what I wanted from it. Now, I love working with*

Thora and I knew she added great value to the business, but at first, I dug in and said to her many times, "It's my business." I know I could not have done it without her. But at the beginning she wasn't a clear partner in the business, so we had to address those issues. I had to come to terms that if I was truly bringing in a partner, I had to let go of the sole owner attitude and allow her to bring her contributions into our company. Years later, I am so glad I did, although I still struggle at times because I am human. I know that it is far better having a partner like Thora than being without her.

When Thora first came into the company, I don't think we could have had the conversation of "what if." We were lucky that we did not need those answers. Now I know how important it is and how it might have helped us to create the exit strategy a few years earlier than we did.

THORA: *I agree. We couldn't have had an exit strategy conversation early in our marriage or early in our time working together. The timing wasn't right until a few years ago.*

When we first started, I was handling the administration and process implementation side of things. I felt like a partner, but at first it was not a legal business partnership. It was more of an understanding, but legally that didn't protect me in any way if anything happened to Sean or our marriage.

When I first started working with him, Sean always said, "This is my business. It is my concept. You work here. It is not yours." It wasn't easy for me to put 100 percent of my energy into the business when my partner wasn't willing to let go of the reins and treat me like an equal. But I also understood the blood, sweat, and tears Sean had put into the company up to that point. He just needed time to see what I could bring to the company and learn to trust my instincts, motives, and actions so he could eventually let down his guard.

CREATING HEALTHY BOUNDARIES

THORA: *It was hard in the early years to wrap my head around a business exit strategy because this was our baby, and the fear of the unknown without that baby to care for was difficult to process. Now it makes sense to theoretically let our baby, which is now grown, go off on its own and make it possible for us to move on to a different phase of life, too.*

Then we eventually got to a level where we could talk about, "Well, if we got divorced, could we still work together, and would we want to?"

In the beginning of our marriage, we were both immature. So we'd say things like, "No way. If we got divorced, we couldn't work together." Now I think our maturity level as business partners has changed so much that if the business demanded it and we were making a lot of money, why wouldn't we at least try to make it work under those terms?

SEAN: *It would be harder to work together as just business partners and not marriage partners, too, but it might be worth working it out for the business.*

The process of creating our exit strategy (2016 to 2020) helped us clarify our boundaries about what each of us wanted to be responsible for in the business. It also outlined what we really wanted out of our companies. We took into consideration each of our personalities, strengths, and skills sets and established a clearer business structure. We came to the conclusion that we could continue running our companies well into our retirement years or we could start to structure the model to sell. We would be OK and prepared for both scenarios should we need or want to make the choice.

As of 2017, we moved into true CEO and COO roles and began to focus on the vision of the company, maintaining the overall standards and foundation that are so vital to our current and future employees. We have created and defined roles that support the company and vision, thus providing a road map that will allow the company to survive and succeed after an exit from ownership. The true entrepreneur's dream: let it live on.

CONSIDERING THE LEGAL AND FINANCIAL "WHAT IFS"

There are other exit strategy topics we discuss that are directly related to the business as well. For example, what is our plan if the business must file for bankruptcy or otherwise dissolve? Who decides what? Who files the legal paperwork? Who does the negotiating? How are any proceeds or debt divided?

When we opened another Club Tattoo studio in San Francisco in 2012, we invested more than $2 million. It was the most beautiful studio we had ever built, and we were certain it would succeed. Unfortunately, the location turned out to be a failure, and we painfully decided to close the studio after three years. (Read more about it in Chapter 13.)

Without an exit strategy, this could have bankrupted us and the entire company. Luckily, we had thought it through prior to opening the studio and put in place a solid exit plan in case things went wrong. As a result, we not only survived after this failure but rebounded and grew the brand again shortly after closing the location.

Another possible legal pitfall is when there is a system or process developed for the business that increases revenue, saves time, or standardizes a process. Any of these might be considered an intellectual property. But who owns it?

Many larger corporations specify in their employee contracts that anything developed by the employee while employed by the corporation will forever be legally considered the intellectual property of the corporation. But in a smaller company, what do you do with a computer technology that an employee or partner develops and brings to the day-to-day business operation?

It is important to remember that a business is a changing, dynamic entity that requires constant adjustment. The bigger it is or the more locations or partners involved, the more you will require clear boundaries in day-to-day operations and clear exit strategies for whatever reason that may arise.

Yes, creating a viable exit strategy might be emotionally and legally difficult to process, but *not* doing it will be much harder to untangle and manage. It's always nice to have good intentions or believe that the person you are dealing with has good intentions, but a clear and concise agreement or contract can help you and others avoid any unnecessary disagreements.

CHAPTER
17

NOW THAT WE'VE MADE IT, WHAT DO WE DO?

S ean's parents struggled financially for most of Sean's childhood but always provided enough for the family to get by. Sean remembers that buying school clothes was always a stressful time in his home because his mom would give them $100 for the entire school year, which barely covered a pair of shoes, two T-shirts, and two or three pairs of pants or shorts. Sean felt ashamed for not having as much as most of the other kids, but his family simply couldn't afford any extras.

This feeling of shame, unfair as it is, is what children put on themselves when they don't yet understand how the world works. Most of the kids around Sean probably had the same financial problems as his family; he just couldn't see it. Growing up this way has always made Sean want to give back to the community. Even when we had nothing, we volunteered to help underprivileged families during the holidays and worked at charitable activities.

Once we started our company, we made it part of our mission to give back, no matter how much we had. We wanted to make a difference in the world and show people that no matter how hard things get, there is always hope, and there are kind people willing to help you help yourselves. As we bring this story of our brand to a close, that's what we want to leave you with: What you do with your brand when you've made it. And for us, the answer is clear: You give back.

GOOD INTENTIONS AREN'T ALWAYS THE BEST INTENTIONS

In 1995, we had our first year at Club Tattoo. Sean was about to turn 22, and as Christmas came around, he noticed a building about ten blocks away from our original location where there were a lot of single moms and children living in what looked like a hotel. It seemed odd for a school bus to be picking kids up from a hotel, so he asked some of the nearby business owners. One of them explained that it was called La Mesita Lodge (now called A New Leaf at La Mesita Apartments), an organization that helped battered women and their children. Sean was interested, and went to the lodge to learn more.

As Sean entered, the staff in the lobby were initially very guarded, but once he talked to them a bit, they opened up and began to tell him about their organization. Their mission was to help women get out of abusive relationships. They had a strong relationship with local police departments, which would contact them after a domestic violence incident so they could send a representative to the police station or hospital (whichever the situation called for) and plead with the woman to get out of the relationship. They would offer to take her and her children to the lodge and let them live there for up to a year, with all food and lodging expenses covered. They would then help train the mother with a skill and offer free childcare while she was learning the skill and getting interviews for her new career.

Then, once they were ready to move out, the lodge would help them find new housing.

As you can imagine, many women in abusive situations find it hard to leave for a variety of reasons: they may be financially dependent on the man they are living with, they may not have a safe place to go, or they may just be too damn afraid of the bastard who is beating them. Whatever the reason, this place was helping them see beyond their immediate situation and offering them hope. Hope is an incredibly powerful gift. As other people besides us have stated, "The world is built on hope."

Sean was hooked. They showed him around the facility, being careful to maintain the anonymity of the women and children who lived there. He could not believe such an organization existed only a few yards away from our business. He asked the facilitator if the lodge needed anything, such as food or clothing, for its residents. She said they operated 100 percent from donations alone; they had been running for several years this way and were growing exponentially thanks to the help of the community.

As Sean left the lodge, he felt that he needed to do something to help, so he scrounged up about $100, went to Target, and bought as much as he could: probably three or four outfits for a woman and two outfits for children around four or five years old. He bought some toiletries like toothbrushes and shampoo to round it out. Sean remembers feeling so proud that he was trying to make a difference as he left the store that he called his mom and told her all about the lodge.

The next day, Sean drove over to the lodge with the donations and met the same lady who had given him the tour the day before. She took him to a little storage room that held racks of clothing and shelves of supplies, told him to put his items there, and then quickly escorted him off the property, as the children were returning from school soon and they wanted the lot cleared of visitors.

SEAN: *I remember feeling really underwhelmed and let down by my experience. I thought that I was going to meet some of the people I had so selflessly helped and that I would get the satisfaction of knowing them—and, more importantly, they would know that I had helped them. None of this felt right.*

It took Sean several months to figure out why he had felt the way he did at the time. It didn't feel right because Sean was not giving from the right place with the right intention. He was giving because he wanted others to know that he was giving. That's not entirely true—he did want to make other people happy—but he wanted them to acknowledge his good deed.

It took a while to understand that what Sean had done wasn't charitable. A true act of charity gives without expectation of acknowledgment or reward. He had to learn that the reward for giving comes from knowing that you helped someone, even if they never know who gave the help.

DON'T DO IT FOR THE GLORY, BUT SHARE IT TO INSPIRE OTHERS

Once Sean understood why he should give to others, he made it a mission to get involved anonymously. Once we were married, we gave together anonymously to the La Mesita Lodge for the next 16 years, until our charity donations/work grew so large we chose to focus the majority of it through A New Leaf Foundation. This was the umbrella that Las Mesita had eventually been brought under. Our entire staff understands the primary function and focus of this charity and realizes its impact on our local battered women/single mothers/ homeless community in our area. Through seeing and contributing through action and Club Tattoo, our team has developed a larger sense of purpose and has now started to give on their own directly. We eventually became a top donor to A New Leaf Foundation and still donate our energy, time, and money to this day.

However, we ultimately changed our perspective on doing it anonymously. As the years passed and Club Tattoo and our other businesses became more successful, we became better known throughout the world as entrepreneurs. Unfortunately, success brings with it enemies who want to see you fail.

We remember attending a conference in Las Vegas in 2010. At one point, Sean saw some friends in a large crowd at one of the casino bars and went up to say hello. He was talking to his friends when he heard a man shouting from across the bar: "You think you're so fucking great with all your success, but you don't give shit back to anyone but yourself! You're just another greedy fucking capitalist!"

It took Sean several moments to understand what he was yelling, and finally someone said, "Are you going to let that dude talk to you like that?" Sean didn't know what to do. When he was younger, he would have knocked the guy's teeth out, but he was in front of colleagues and knew that would only make him look worse. Looking back, Sean was more hurt that the guy was saying these things, given how much we regularly did to give back to our community.

That was the moment we decided that we would let others know what we did to give back—not because we wanted their approval, but because we wanted to start inspiring the people around us to start giving back as well. We started to post our community activities through our social media channels and website, and get our employees involved in them. It began to work just as we had hoped. Our staff saw us giving, so they wanted to give, and then our clients started to give as well.

GET YOUR STAFF INVOLVED

We eventually started to donate time with our staff to an organization called Feed My Starving Children. This organization is AMAZING! They have a facility in Mesa that is open to members of the public who want to donate their time and energy. We asked our staff if any of them would like to join us and had 14 employees on our first outing. We didn't know what to expect our first time, but it was inspiring and amazing.

The organization briefly summed up its mission, which is to, you guessed it, feed starving children in impoverished nations around the globe. They do so by packing meals in a highly organized fashion and shipping them all over the world. They gave us a rundown of how we were to work in groups to pack the meals and then sent us into the facility.

It lasted about 60 to 90 minutes and was some of the most fun we had ever had volunteering. An added benefit was the enormous bonding and team-building impact it had on our staff. They couldn't wait to do it again, and it has become part of our company culture to give back to our community in this way. Our staff and clients have now brought their friends and families onboard, and the cycle of giving continues to this day.

In Las Vegas, we found a similar organization called Three Square. They work within the greater community of Las Vegas and provide meals for more than 50,000 people every month. This organization was founded by members of the Hilton Hotel family and has expanded from its first year in 2007 into a monster charity. The facility they have built and the team members who manage it are truly awe-inspiring.

In 2019, our Club Tattoo team was able to donate generously to A New Leaf Foundation, Feed My Starving Children, and Three Square, all reliable and worthy partners in helping the Arizona and Las Vegas communities. It has given us a new sense of purpose and truly makes us feel like we are making a difference in the world, not only by giving what we can but also by inspiring others to step up and take action.

We have decided to take on the mission of giving back to those in need around the world, whether that is an orphanage in Mexico, a homeless shelter in Arizona, or simply hungry children in various countries around the world. Helping others has become a privilege that we both enjoy on a daily basis.

RENEGADE GRATITUDE

Since we created and founded Club Tattoo in 1995, we have learned much and continue to grow as a father and a husband, a mother and a wife, partners, and business owners. We firmly believe that we will never stop learning from others and each other, and that life in essence is one giant lesson. We are forever grateful to our parents, grandparents, family, and our mentors for everything they have given us.

We have created a successful business that is now worth tens of millions of dollars. We are considered by many to have the most successful tattoo and piercing studios in the world. We have created more than 130 jobs, and we believe our staff are happy working for and with our companies. We would like to think that we have innovated and had a positive impact on the tattoo and piercing industry. In addition, we have helped thousands of people throughout their careers.

We have what many people consider "the finer things in life," but we have finally gotten to a place where we don't evaluate our success based on how much money we have accumulated or the number of properties we own. We threw out those measuring sticks a long time ago. Now we chart our progress in the world based on how many people we have fed, sheltered, and clothed and on how much we give to charity.

Our vision of personal success lies in how we treat and love each other and our family. The only real "stuff" we like to spend our money on these days is traveling the world with our kids and each other. Experiences are the only things we can take with us, so those are still investments worth making.

The world needs more role models and fewer critics. Push your fellow humans into fulfilling the potential you know they have. Everyone needs a confidence booster, someone who believes in their ability to overcome obstacles. You never know whose life you can impact, or how much it can be affected, by a simple "You can do this" vote of confidence.

We've been told many times that we are very lucky. We were in fact lucky to be born in the United States. There is no other country that affords the opportunities that this one does. That is not meant as an insult to any other country. We have traveled the world, but in our minds and hearts, we feel blessed to have been born and brought up here. We are blessed in that we can use our talents and strengths to pursue the opportunities available to us. We also believe that in a business context, luck is just being ready when an opportunity comes along. Being prepared means that you are willing to do the necessary work at that moment. It also means being willing to take the risks required for success and moving forward despite your fear.

Most obstacles are in your mind, and you can overcome anything you put your mind to. Most times, it takes having an obstacle in your life for you to grow. It is the very act of overcoming those problems that gives your life meaning and purpose. Without that, life would be boring, and nobody wants that. We're not pretending that struggles are fun—of course not. But you should recognize that those moments of conflict are the point at which you can learn and become a better version of yourself.

Positive affirmation can help you get through tough situations. Consistently tell yourself that you can and will succeed in what you are trying to do, and eventually your mind will believe it. Visualize yourself succeeding. Think about what your task will look like when it's complete and perfect. Hold that image in your mind for when things get hard, and it will help you push through. This exercise really does work. When your mind begins to believe that you can do something, it will find a way to make it happen.

We really do live in the greatest country in the world, even with all its faults. We are profoundly grateful for that, and we should never take it for granted. There is no excuse for failing, given all the socioeconomic and environmental advantages that we have in this country. We challenge each and every one of you who live in it to go out and take the opportunity to make your entrepreneurial dreams come true. Make a difference in your life and the lives of others.

Work hard, inspire others, and never stop trying. Be proud and reap the rewards of doing so. Here are ten simple reminders that we have used on our brand renegade journey for our business growth and personal happiness:

1. Be mindful of the benefits of finding the right mentor who will push you to accomplish your goals and dreams!

2. If you are ready, become a mentor to someone who needs what you can offer.

3. Do what you say you will. Your word is your bond. Keep an open dialogue with your customers to find out their changing needs and wants.

4. Be consistent in your approach and flexible in your methods.

5. Be willing to learn. Get comfortable making affordable mistakes.

6. Take calculated risks. Don't be so afraid to fail that you don't try. Failure is part of your journey—accept it, learn from it, and keep moving forward. It is always better to have tried and failed than to never try and wonder "what could have happened."

7. Keep your focus on digging down, refining your brand, and curating a unique customer experience. Your brand message is just as important as what you are selling. Make sure it is clear and gives your prospective customers a glimpse of what your company stands for, is, or is not. Be who you say you are.

8. Be kind to others. Give back at all times, whether or not you are wealthy. Giving a piece of yourself, whether that consists of money, time, or energy, matters to those who need it. Giving to others helps define who you are at your core and gives you purpose in life. A fun way of looking at this is to try to be the person that your pets think you are.

9. Be a better boss by becoming a better leader and mentor to others. You are raising the next generation of entrepreneurs. Be kind and open to new ideas and share your knowledge with others.

10. Sometimes, taking that first step is all you need to create the momentum for something great. If you focus on only the negative things that might happen and ignore all the

potential upsides, you may be losing out on something special. Take that first step, say "Fuck it," and do it anyway!

Lastly, business should be fun. If you don't enjoy what you're doing, go out and find something you love. Chase your passion and enjoy the time you have on this earth. Time is never promised, and we are all here for a short amount of it. Make yours count and leave nothing on the table at the end. No regrets.

ACKNOWLEDGMENTS

We would like to thank our parents, Willie Lue Payne and Kathy and Cameron Dowdell; Carston and Brennen, for being the best kids we could hope for; Bob Parsons, Tom Whalley, and Debbie Allen; Chester Bennington, for being such a great partner and friend for so long; and Gregg Paul.

ABOUT THE AUTHORS

Since Club Tattoo started in 1995, Sean and Thora Dowdell have worked together to grow it into seven locations and a multimillion-dollar tattoo and piercing business, with locations in the Phoenix area and Las Vegas. They have been married 22 years and have two sons. They have worked together as full business partners, spouses, and parents who are successful on all fronts.

Sean and Thora have created many innovations in their field, including two patents for software and jewelry design. They have made several worldwide licensing and collaboration deals with other renowned brands, including Oster, Bicycle Cards, Etnies, *Women's Wear Daily*, Nordstrom, The Venetian Resort, Caesars Entertainment, Boldface Gear, and many more. Many people might say they have survived against great odds to build a multimillion-dollar business in an industry that was not looking to be re-created or mainstreamed. Sean and Thora have also overcome the odds against them with regard to the almost 50 percent divorce rate in the United States, which is even higher for couples who attempt to build a business together.

Sean is known as the Tattooed Millionaire, which is also the title of his first book, published in May 2017. Sean is well-respected in his community and industry and is connected with many leaders and innovators in other industries as well. Over the past several years, Sean has been interviewed for a wide variety of magazines and other media, including *Entrepreneur* magazine, *GQ*, *Billboard*, *Success*, *The Washington Post*, *Parade* magazine, *Rolling Stone*, *Reader's Digest*, *Spin*, *Kerrang!*, *Revolver*, *Los Angeles Times*, *Las Vegas Weekly*, *HuffPost*, and *BuzzFeed*, among many others. He has been featured on many TV shows and stations, including CNBC, ABC, NBC, CNN, VICE, and A&E; on NPR radio; and made guest appearances on podcasts including *The Adam Carolla Show*, NPR, *Inspired Media 360*, and many more.

It's not fair or accurate to call Thora the quieter or secondary of the two business partners, although she has been less front and center in the media than Sean in the past. However, Thora is stepping out to speak up more often about her personal and business journey. Thora is a full business partner and the force behind developing and expanding the Club Tattoo brand into the multimillion-dollar enterprise it is today. She created and implemented, and still fine-tunes and updates, the business systems and processes that allow Club Tattoo to run profitably and successfully. She works tirelessly to protect the interests of the owners and the employees, from the front of the shop to the back, as well as providing a consistent, comfortable, and professional customer experience.

While Thora has not yet made a big push into the public speaking arena, she is loved and listened to when she does take the stage. She is beginning to embrace more opportunities to share her business insight, especially when it comes to empowering women business owners who may have heard, "No, you can't do that," "You're not smart enough," or "Who do you think you are?"

One of the topics Thora wants to share more with women already in business and young girls just starting out is her belief that "'I can' is more powerful than IQ." Having grown up in a male-dominated world and been told "no" more times than she wants to remember, Thora has learned that she gets to decide what she wants to do and can find or learn a way to do it. She is self-taught, self-motivated, and a force to be reckoned with personally and professionally.

INDEX

CPSIA information can be obtained
at www.ICGtesting.com
Printed in the USA
JSHW020137030521
13937JS00002B/2